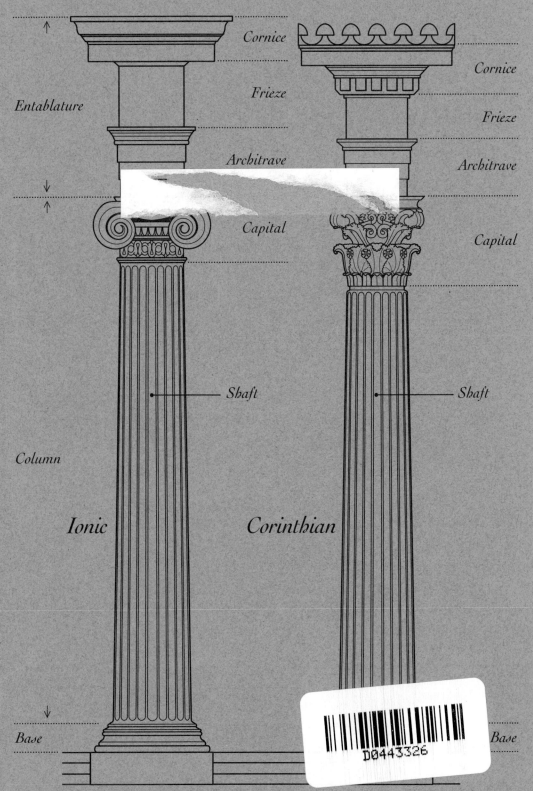

OF GRECIAN ARCHITECTURE

Cornice

Frieze

Architrave

Capital

Entablature

Cornice

Frieze

Architrave

Capital

Shaft

Shaft

Column

Ionic

Corinthian

Base

Base

From Peter Nicholson's *The New and Improved Practical Builder* (1848), redrawn by Donna DeVore Pritchett 1996

CLASSICAL
NASHVILLE

CLASSICAL NASHVILLE

Athens of  *the South*

by

Christine Kreyling

Wesley Paine

Charles W. Warterfield, Jr.

Susan Ford Wiltshire

with an essay by
Alan LeQuire, sculptor of the Nashville Athena

Book and jacket design by Gary Gore

VANDERBILT UNIVERSITY PRESS

Nashville and London

Library of Congress Cataloging-in-Publication Data

Classical Nashville : Athens of the South / by
Christine Kreyling . . . [et al.] : with an essay by Alan
LeQuire.—1st ed.
       p.   cm.   .
Includes bibliographical references and index.
ISBN 0-8265-1277-1 (alk. paper)
       1. Nashville (Tenn.)—Civilization.   2. United
States—Civilization—Classical influences.
I. Kreyling, Christine, 1949–   .

F444.N25C58   1996   96-12087
976.8'55—dc20   CIP

Contents

Acknowledgments

As the identity of a city evolves out of the vision and work of many people, so did this book. We acknowledge with gratitude the contributions of the following individuals.

Among our advisors were a number of scholars of the history of Nashville who themselves have contributed significantly to that history: Wilbur Creighton, Don H. Doyle, John Egerton, State Senator Douglas Henry, Kem Hinton, Alice Keeble, Robert McGaw, Margaret Lindsley Warden, and Ridley Wills.

Ophelia Paine of the Metropolitan Historical Commission and Carol Farrah Kaplan of the Nashville Room of the Ben West Public Library read much of the manuscript and saved us from many errors.

James A. Hoobler, curator of the Tennessee State Capitol, supplied and confirmed historical data. Nicholas Gianopolous of Philadelphia, an expert on William Strickland, sent us photographs of the two Strickland buildings in Philadelphia that appear in this volume. M. Carr Payne, Jr., provided first-hand knowledge of the planning of the Peabody campus.

Deborah Hutchison patiently assisted with transferring numerous hand-written pages into the computer. Tommye Corlew, secretary of the Department of Classical Studies at Vanderbilt University, facilitated communication among multiple authors and occasionally provided research assistance.

Marilyn Hughes of the Tennessee State Library and Archives and John Anderson of the Texas State Archives

Prints and Photographs Collections generously located and provided illustrations.

The staff of the Nashville Parthenon, including Vechelle Brown, Timothy Cartmell, Bobby Lawrence, Gary Pace, Susan Shockley, and especially Liz Gold, joined together to support our endeavor.

Madeleine J. Goodman, Dean of the College of Arts and Science of Vanderbilt University, granted a research leave of absence that helped bring this book to conclusion. Vanderbilt colleagues who provided valuable advice include Leonard Folgarait and Barbara Tsakirgis. A number of Vanderbilt students at various stages contributed research assistance and enthusiasm to this project: David Beaird, Richard H. Davis, Mary Helen Harvey, Jon Parish Peede, and Helen Pryor.

Family members who provided aesthetic sensibility as well as good judgment include David Paine, Harding Paine, Michael Kreyling, and Ashley T. Wiltshire.

We gratefully acknowledge the director and staff of the Vanderbilt University Press, who attended the publication of this volume with their accustomed professionalism and unfailing good will.

Finally, we extend our warmest appreciation to Ann Reynolds, executive director of the Metropolitan Historical Commission, who brought the four of us together before we knew there was a book.

Prelude

In a Nashville neighborhood east of the Cumberland River, a teacher steps out onto a wide porch, its low roof supported by Ionic columns, to retrieve the morning newspaper.

Downtown, two lawmakers hurry from the Hermitage Hotel across Legislative Plaza to an early meeting at the Capitol. As they pass the massive Doric colonnade of the War Memorial Building, the sun ricocheting off the bronze statue of Victory inside the portico catches their eyes.

An early-morning jogger in Centennial Park slows to admire the east pediment of the Nashville Parthenon. A visitor to the city, he climbs the high steps and turns toward downtown. Due east he sees the Greek-style Tennessee State Capitol, framed in the light of the morning sun.

Farther to the west on Harding Road, two architectural historians stand in the early light in front of the Belle Meade Mansion, reviewing their drawings of its imposing pilastered facade one more time before heading to the airport.

Another day is underway in Music City USA—the Athens of the South.

Nashville as Athens

The city is the teacher of its people.

SIMONIDES
5th century B.C.

F or all its prominence, most visitors and many Nashvillians do not know why a full-scale replica of the ancient Greek Parthenon in Athens was built in Nashville, or why it is a symbol of the city. By the end of the nineteenth century the identification of Nashville with classical Athens was so ingrained in the popular imagination that choosing a replica of the Parthenon as Nashville's centerpiece for the Tennessee Centennial Exposition in 1897 seemed a natural thing to do. The identity of Nashville as the "Athens of the South" had much earlier origins, but the term became official when Tennessee Governor Bob Taylor used it in his speech at the opening of the Exposition.

Nashville assumed a classical character almost from its origins because of the distinctiveness of the city's history. Nashville was founded in the 1780s when a taste for classical architecture was first appearing in the eastern United States, a taste formed by admiration for Greek democracy and Roman republicanism. The older cities on the eastern seaboard, however, were already well established in other architectural styles, while Nashville grew into a city at the height of the interest in classicism.

Nashville was also a frontier town, at one point the largest

English-speaking community west of the Appalachians. As the political center of the southwest territory, it was conscious of its potential as well as of the differences that distinguished it from the more settled portions of the country. Its leaders saw the opportunity to dignify their endeavors by adapting classical tastes to a frontier setting.

The most important reason for the identification of Nashville with classical Athens, however, lies squarely in the city's early commitment to education. In the frighteningly cold winter of 1780, John Donelson led some three hundred settlers, including women and children, on flatboats on the thousand-mile journey down the Holston to the Tennessee, down the Tennessee to the Ohio, up the Ohio to the Cumberland, and finally up the Cumberland to the present site of Nashville. During the journey, classes were held for the children on board.

The previous fall James Robertson's party of some two hundred men plus livestock had set out on land from North Carolina. Other parties, including families with children, joined them along the way. They came up through Virginia, westward along the Wilderness Trail, through the Cumberland Gap into Kentucky, and finally south into Tennessee and the site Robertson had selected the previous summer. When the Donelson's flatboats arrived on April 24, 1780, the combined group framed the Cumberland Compact for the governance of the new community.

The first priority for the settlers was to clear the forests by the banks of the Cumberland and to secure the surroundings. Soon, however, James Robertson was traveling back to Raleigh, North Carolina, to persuade the state legislature to charter an academy in Nashville. His bill, entered in the North Carolina legislature in 1785, led to the founding of Davidson Academy—later known as Cumberland College and later still as the University of Nashville. General public education would not come until the middle of the nineteenth century, as it did elsewhere in the country, but the many private academies and colleges were testimonials to the settlers' commitment to education.

From the city's early days, the study of the classical languages held a central place in Nashville's educational and some of its religious institutions. This commitment was not taken lightly. The issue of knowledge of the classical languages caused a schism in the Presbyterian church, leading to the founding of a new denomination only a few miles from Nashville in the early nineteenth century. At Roger Williams University and Fisk University, both founded shortly after the Civil War, education based on the classical languages was seen as "liberal education" in the true sense, the key to intellectual freedom and equality for former slaves. At Vanderbilt University, Latin was required for election to the academic honorary fraternity Phi Beta Kappa. A circle of Vanderbilt poets known as the Fugitives, including John Crowe Ransom, Allen Tate, and Robert Penn Warren, found a way to move beyond the literary preoccupation of the Old South and its nostalgia for the days of slavery by adapting classical themes to universalize their work.

Three individuals in the early history of Nashville were especially conspicuous in moving the city toward classical ideas: Andrew Jackson, Philip Lindsley, and William Strickland. Politically the most prominent was Jackson. His patronage of classical architecture—in both the second and final versions of The Hermitage, as well as in Tulip Grove, the home he commissioned for his wife's nephew—gave official weight to classicism as a local style for building.

The person most responsible for the specific identification of Nashville with classical Athens was Philip Lindsley, president of the University of Nashville from 1825 to 1850. Lindsley, a native of New Jersey who had been a classics professor at Princeton University before accepting the presidency of the fledgling college in the west, was exceedingly ambitious both for the University of Nashville and for his adopted city. Some historians credit him with using the term "Athens of the West" in speeches as early as 1840.[1] The term, however, is fully documented for the first time in 1859 when Lindsley's former student and biographer Leroy J. Halsey wrote of him:

But perhaps the most striking illustration of his influence as an educator is seen at Nashville itself—the scene of his longest labors, the home of his adoption, the resting-place where his ashes sleep. We have no citizenship at Nashville; and hence cannot be accused of partiality in what we are about to say. But of all we have seen and known, we may safely say, there is no city west of the mountains which seem [sic] to us so justly entitled to be called the "Athens of the West" as Nashville. And for that distinction we think there is no man to whom Nashville is so much indebted as Dr. Lindsley.[2]

In Nashville the emphasis on classical education was followed by a striking preference for public architecture in classical styles. The key figure in shaping the statement made by Nashville's public buildings was William Strickland, one of the nation's leading architects of classicism. By the time the cornerstone of the Tennessee State Capitol was laid on July 4, 1845, the association of Nashville with Athens was firmly in the minds of those who sought to translate educational aspiration into stone.

This aspiration led to the conscious choice to bring Strickland from Philadelphia to design the Capitol. Strickland fashioned a building that articulated in three dimensions what an Athenian style could contribute to public life. He chose a temple form topped with a Greek monument for the new Tennessee Capitol, rather than the Roman dome of the U.S. Capitol and most of the state capitol designs, because of his belief that the proportions of Greek temples represented eternal principles of wisdom, strength, and beauty.

All of this lay behind the choice of the Parthenon as Nashville's contribution to the Tennessee Centennial Exposition in 1897. (For economic and other reasons, the Exposition was postponed until May 1897, following the 1896 centennial of Tennessee statehood.) The original replica of the Parthenon, constructed of brick, lath, and plaster, was rebuilt in more permanent materials in the 1920s. The reconstruction of the Parthenon was made more accurate and striking with the re-creation by Nashville sculptor Alan LeQuire of Pheidias's original monumental statue of Athena Parthenos. The Nashville Athena, nearly forty-two feet tall, was unveiled in 1990.

In a numerical sense, Nashville's most pervasive classical legacy lies not in the public arenas of education and architecture but in the unlikely quarter of the city's suburbs. There, the private home still sounds the theme established by Strickland, that the values of permanence and stability are best upheld by columns and capitals. It is true that some of these classical houses, such as the Hermitage and Belle Meade, have, because of their histories, become public monuments. Others, though far more modest in scale, continue to provide a reassuring shelter from the constant flux of modern life.

Nashville has been a city of paradoxes from the beginning. First a frontier city, it then became a southern city. It sided with the Confederacy in the Civil War, yet many of its leading families had Northern sympathies. Long a racially segregated city, it provided significant leadership to the movements that brought the end of segregation. It is simultaneously a home base for traditional religious institutions and a testing place for innovations in art, intellectual inquiry, and forms of music. Nashville is centered in a web of often-competing contradictions because of its geography as well, located as it is between the Appalachians and the Mississippi, between the states of the North and the Deep South. In all the activities that comprise civic life—education, governance, regional loyalties, racial attitudes, the proper forms of economic development, public and private architecture, the place of literature, music, and the arts—contrasting instincts and energies have played in counterpoint from the early years of the city's history.

Consistent through all of Nashville's history, however, has been the classical Greek ideal of education, art, and community participation that early caused the city to be known as the Athens of the West and, with the eventual population of the territory beyond the Mississippi, as the Athens of the South. It is rare for individuals to be fully aware of the factors that form their identity and sense of self. It is far rarer when the self-ascribed identity of a city can be traced back to its earliest beginnings. In the case of Nashville it is possible to trace how that identity came about, what architectural forms it has taken in our public and private lives, and how a classical spirit continues to inform the atmosphere and ethos of Nashville as the city approaches the twenty-first century.

The identification of Nashville as the Athens of the South has not been without skeptics. J. S. Buckingham, an English traveler to Nashville in 1841, expressed reserve about the claims to classical culture in this frontier west of the Appalachians:

Though the farmers of Tennessee may have their country studded with such classical names as Athens, Sparta, Troy, Carthage, Memphis, and Palmyra . . . it will take some time before their prose compositions will equal those of Demosthenes, or their poetry rival that of Homer; there being only one feature in which they resemble the Athenians—though it must be admitted on much more slender grounds—namely, that of thinking themselves the only polished and refined people on the earth.[3]

Nashville author John Egerton takes a more balanced view in his description of contemporary Nashville. Referring to "Music City USA," a phrase adopted by the Chamber of Commerce in 1978, Egerton writes: "Somewhere between 'the Athens of the West' and 'Music City USA,' between the grime of a railroad town and the glitz of Opryland, between Robert Penn Warren and Robert Altman [director of the 1975 movie *Nashville*], the real Nashville stutters and hums along on a mix of high-octane image and unleaded reality."[4]

Image and reality blend in Nashville because the city's classical identifications from the beginning have been not antiquarian but forward-looking: ambitious, democratic, entrepreneurial, and culturally substantive. These dynamic rather than nostalgic appropriations of classical antiquity suggest that the continuities of classical ideals in present-day Nashville serve not as monuments to a lost past but as sources of energy, creativity, and imagination for the future of a city.

CLASSICAL
NASHVILLE

I

Learning, Religion, and Literature
The Classical Connections

Nashville had nurtured us. We cherished
The heritage it gave us . . .
An Athens in the west before the Parthenon.

FUGITIVE POET JESSE WILLS[1]

ashville is a city where classical learning and tastes have flourished—often improbably, given its frontier origins and later middle-America setting—for a variety of reasons. One is the character of the early settlers and the schools they established. Another is the role of the Presbyterian church in early Nashville and the marked commitment of that religious tradition to education. Universities founded here, including two significant institutions for African-Americans, based their curriculum on classical models and embodied both intellectual rigor and the democratic values of classical Athens.

Those democratic values are reflected in the first Constitution of the State of Tennessee, which was signed in Knoxville on February 6, 1796, in preparation for the admission of Tennessee to statehood on June 1, 1796. This document, says one observer, "is admitted to be one of the very best—Mr. Jefferson said, 'the least imperfect and most republican'—of the systems of government adopted by any of the American States."[2] The consistent commitment of

1

Tennesseans to individual rights and grassroots democracy, which always depend on education, is evident in the fact that Article 1 begins with an extensive Declaration of Rights. Section 1 then reads, "That all power is inherent in the people, and all free governments are founded on their authority, and instituted for their peace, safety, and happiness; for the advancement of those ends they have at all times, an unalienable and indefeasible right to alter, reform, or abolish the government in such manner as they may think proper."[3] The civic tone inherited ultimately from ancient Athens was set from the beginning.

Nashville may have become "the Athens of the South" for more intangible reasons as well, including its stubborn insistence on doing the more difficult, improbable, and therefore more interesting thing—an attitude that provides a wider imaginative perspective than the narrow confines of immediate experience. One example of such contrariness is Sam Houston, an early governor of Tennessee and a man who loved the classics even though he had little formal schooling. Another is the Fugitives, a group of poets nourished by Nashville in the 1920s, who appropriated classical themes as one of their strategies for moving literature beyond Southern regionalism. Their stories begin and end this chapter.

Sam Houston and the Iliad

Sam Houston was born in Rockbridge County, Virginia, on March 2, 1793, then moved as a young boy with his family to East Tennessee. He met Andrew Jackson during the Creek War, so winning the older man's respect for his bravery and character that they formed a lifelong friendship. In 1818 Houston came to Nashville and entered the law offices of James Trimble; eventually he opened his own office on Market Street. Attracted to a career in public service, he was elected to Congress in 1823. Four years later Houston was elected governor of Tennessee and was inaugurated on October 1, 1827.

Houston came to public life filled with the romantic

sense of classical heroism and literary tastes he developed in his childhood. As a boy in east Tennessee, young Houston demanded of his teacher in the local academy that he be taught the ancient languages. When the teacher refused, Sam declared that he would never recite another lesson again, turned on his heel, and left to live for three years with Chief Jolly and his band of Cherokees on an island where the Hiwassee River merges with the Big Tennessee. When his

1.1 "Sam Houston – Paint Me As Marius"
Photograph courtesy Archives Division – Texas State Library

3

brothers finally found him, Houston replied that he "liked the wild liberty of the Red men, better than the tyranny of his own brothers, and if he could not study Latin in the Academy, he could, at least, read a translation from the Greek in the woods, and read it in peace."

He had got possession, in some way, of two or three books, which had a great power over his imagination. No boy ever reads well, till he feels a thirst for intelligence: and no surer indication is needed that this period has come, than to see the mind directed towards those gigantic heroes who rise like spectres from the ruins of Greece and Rome, towering high and clear above the darkness and gloom of the Middle Ages. He had, among other works, Pope's [translation of the] Iliad, *which he read so constantly, we have been assured on the most reliable authority, he could repeat it almost entire from beginning to end.*[4]

Another biographer writes: "Students of Homer, Demosthenes, Euripides, Aeschylus, or Sophocles, probably never gathered more of the classic lore from their authors in the original, than Sam Houston extracted from Pope's translation of the *Iliad.*"[5] In his biography of Houston, Robert Penn Warren insists on the importance of classical texts in Houston's development: "His head was full of ambition to read Homer. He carried into the wilderness a copy of Pope's translation of the *Iliad.* . . . Homer and the wilderness—they gave shape to, and fed, his dream of greatness."[6]

When Sam Houston eventually turned to a political career, he did not abandon his enthusiasm for education or for those he knew were shaping the young country's educational goals. When elected to Congress from the Davidson district in 1823, Houston left for Washington with a letter of introduction from his friend Andrew Jackson to Thomas Jefferson, founder of the University of Virginia and at that time a member of the school board of Albemarle County. Later, in his first address to the Tennessee Legislature after inauguration as governor in 1827, Houston set out a program for the state that centered on plans to establish a permanent fund in support of public schools.[7]

Dreams of heroic action persisted throughout Houston's life. In his first address to Congress, he compared Andrew Jackson with Cincinnatus gone back to his plow. As president of Texas, he compared the men who died at the Alamo with Leonidas and his Spartans at Thermopylae. In the fight for the Compromise of 1850 he spoke of Henry Clay as "the Ajax whose battle axe glistened aloft in the thickest of the fight."[8] During a brief visit to Nashville from Indian country in 1831, where he had gone after his abrupt resignation as governor of Tennessee, he commissioned a painting of himself as Marius, the Roman consul who many times came back from defeats he had suffered (fig. 1.1).

Sam Houston's passion for the classics in a frontier setting characterized many settlers in Tennessee from the time of their earliest arrival. For most of those, that passion was cultivated not in the woods but in the more traditional settings of school and church.

The Beginnings and the First Schools

Even before John Donelson and his band of flatboat settlers arrived at the place they knew as "French Lick," one of their party, a certain Reuben Harrison, went ashore to hunt and did not return in the evening to the boat. Donelson writes:

Friday 3rd: Early in the morning fired a four pounder for the lost man, sent out sundry persons to search the woods for him, firing many guns that day and the succeeding night, but all without success, to the great grief of his parents and fellow travellers "vale! vale!"[9]

The passengers on the flatboat *Adventure* knew the Latin form of "farewell." Happily this proved not to be a final farewell, as the lost Mr. Harrison was eventually found and restored to safety.

The level of education among the early settlers was

remarkably high: Of the 250 men who signed the Cumberland Compact in April 1780, only one had to sign his name with an "X." The concern for education was evident, too, from the classes taught during the winter voyage on the flatboats in 1780 by Mrs. Ann Johnston, the widowed sister of James Robertson. After the landing at the site that would become Nashville, Mrs. Johnston continued teaching the children.

Soon after Davidson County was founded, a school was established to educate the inhabitants. On December 29, 1785, the North Carolina Legislature passed an act called "An Act for the Promotion of Learning in the County of Davidson." In 1785, even though Nashville was no more than a few buildings, the North Carolina legislature chartered and granted 240 acres of land as an endowment for Davidson Academy. President of the Board of Trustees for the academy was Reverend Thomas B. Craighead, a Presbyterian minister from North Carolina and a 1775 graduate of Nassau Hall at Princeton, New Jersey.

Reverend Craighead arrived on a Saturday afternoon early in 1785. The next day, he climbed up on a tree stump and preached the first Presbyterian sermon heard in Nashville.[10] Later he became the first minister of the First Presbyterian Church in Nashville.

Davidson Academy, the school that became the University of Nashville, was founded by the Reverend Craighead on Gallatin Road where the Spring Hill cemetery is now located. Later it moved across the Cumberland River to College Street, now Third Avenue South. Its destiny—and much of Nashville's classical future—was to lie in the hands of another man from Princeton.

Philip Lindsley (1786–1855) was born in Morristown, New Jersey, and was ten years old when Tennessee became the sixteenth state to join the Union. In 1813 Lindsley was appointed professor of Greek and Latin at Princeton University; in 1822 he was made vice president and then acting president of the University in 1823. The following year

Lindsley turned down the presidency of Princeton to accept the presidency of Cumberland College, soon to be renamed the University of Nashville, in Nashville, Tennessee, a thousand miles to the southwest (fig. 1.2).

In October of 1824 Lindsley set out overland on the seventy-day journey with his wife and four small children, arriving in Nashville on December 24. It was the year Andrew Jackson first ran for president, and Nashville was a center of political activity, the leading city on the southwestern frontier.

Also an ordained Presbyterian minister, Philip Lindsley was committed to education generally and especially to the need for educational institutions in the "Southwest." In a circular letter to his friends explaining his move he wrote: "Throughout the immense valley of the lower Mississippi, containing at least a million of inhabitants, there exists not a single college." Lindsley's vigorous leadership and vision, undiminished by failed hopes of state and private aid to his institution, were shared by others in this frontier setting. By 1848 twenty colleges had been founded in Tennessee.

1.2 Philip Lindsley (Illman Brothers engraving)
Collection of Margaret Lindsley Warden.
Photograph: Charles W. Warterfield, Jr.

The credit for establishing Nashville as an important educational center belongs to Lindsley. Over the next twenty-five years he developed a remarkably accomplished faculty in the University of Nashville, attracted able students to the new university, and turned down the presidency of six other institutions to continue his work in Nashville.[11] His writings on education were widely disseminated, and his leadership extended also to church matters. In 1834 he became moderator of the Presbyterian General Assembly.

Philip Lindsley believed devoutly that every human being is entitled to an education as a rightful inheritance. He saw education as a good in itself, as a great equalizer, and as the special right of the poor. "Learning," he wrote, "is itself a treasure—an estate—of which no adverse fortune can ever deprive its possessor."[12]

On social issues, too, Lindsley was a man of vision and courage. In one of his early essays entitled "Thoughts on Slavery," he states plainly: "Our slaves must be emancipated."

Lindsley's son, John Berrien Lindsley (1822-1897), was two years old when his parents and three young siblings set out on their long trek to Nashville. John Berrien Lindsley was graduated from the University of Nashville in 1839, then received an M.D. from the University of Pennsylvania in 1843. In 1850 he founded the medical department of the University of Nashville and served as its dean for six years.

In 1852, the city council of Nashville engaged a leading citizen and educator, Alfred Hume, to visit the best public school systems in several Northern cities to prepare a plan for public schools in Nashville. Hume observed schools in Philadelphia and elsewhere but modeled his plan especially on the Boston public school system. The plan he advocated called for a board of education that would elect a superintendent and teachers, set salaries, and plan the course of studies. Among the subjects of the high school, along with advanced mathematics and science, were instruction in modern French and Spanish, as well as classical Latin, Greek, and Hebrew. Nashville's first public school, named for Hume and based on his recommendations, opened two and a half years later, on February 26, 1855.[13]

In the meantime, sufficient funding for public schools in the state had been achieved through the leadership of Governor Andrew Johnson. In his message to the state legislature in 1853, Johnson proclaimed that the only way to secure adequate funding for the state's public schools, which had begged in vain for funding, was to levy and collect taxes from the people of the entire state. Johnson, who had learned to read as an adult, was able to surmount stiff opposition to his measure, and direct taxation was passed by the legislature on February 28, 1853.[14]

In 1855 John Berrien Lindsley became Chancellor of the University of Nashville, with which the medical department had fully merged. When the college division closed during the Civil War, the medical school stayed open, and Lindsley was in charge of the Confederate hospitals in Nashville until the Union forces occupied the city in 1862 after the battle of Nashville.

After the war John Berrien Lindsley exercised leadership in an astonishing array of activities. He worked in public health through four cholera epidemics in Nashville, later serving as public health officer and, in the same years 1876–1880, as secretary of the state board of health. Earlier he had committed himself to developing a strong system of public education in Nashville, first as a member of the local board of education (1856-1860), then in 1866 as superintendent of schools. From 1875-1887 he served as secretary of the state board of education. In 1855 Lindsley had brought the Western Military Institute to Nashville as part of the University of Nashville. The will of Montgomery Bell, who died in that same year, left $20,000 to the University of Nashville for scholarships for underprivileged boys. After the war, Lindsley took the money left by Bell, by then $60,000, and opened Montgomery Bell Academy in 1867.

In 1875 with the help of the Peabody Education Fund, Lindsley turned the University of Nashville into an institution for the training of teachers. After 1889 it was renamed Peabody Normal College and in 1905 became known as the George Peabody College for Teachers. The College retained its independence until it became part of Vanderbilt University in 1979. The study of Latin was considered fundamental by both Philip and John Berrien Lindsley in all their educational endeavors, and a Ph.D. in Latin was offered at Peabody College until the mid-1940s.

Like his father, John Berrien Lindsley was also an ordained Presbyterian clergyman. After serving for twenty-

9

four years as a minister of the Presbyterian Church in the United States of America, he joined the Cumberland Presbyterian Church in 1870 because he considered its theology and social spirit more progressive.[15]

The contributions of other members of the Lindsley family continued to support the claim of Nashville as "Athens of the South." John Berrien Lindsley's daughter, Louise Grundy Lindsley (1858–1944), a woman of imposing presence, social conscience, and leadership skills, organized the Ladies Hermitage Association and worked long and hard for the Southern Commercial Congress, the motto of which was "A Greater Nation Through a Greater South." She was, in addition, an untiring activist for social betterment through the Housewives' League and similar organizations.

Louise Grundy Lindsley also created an early form of continuing adult education. On October 16, 1917, the New York paper *The Evening Mail* called her the "Moonlight Lady" of Tennessee because of her successful plan to open country schoolhouses on moonlit nights, when adult men and women who had had little opportunity for education could make their way to evening classes taught by educated women who volunteered for the project.[16]

The Wallace University School was founded in 1885 to serve as a preparatory school for Vanderbilt University. The founders called Clarence B. Wallace, a graduate of Hampden-Sydney and the University of Virginia, to come as headmaster. Mr. Wallace retained this position until the school was closed in 1942. Originally located on 6th Avenue South, the school moved to West End Avenue across from the Cathedral of the Incarnation. Mr. Wallace exerted a powerful influence on his students and inculcated not only classical learning but also Presbyterian virtues.

Graduates of Mr. Wallace's school include the sportswriter Grantland Rice, a native of Murfreesboro and Vanderbilt graduate in 1901; Fugitive poet Jesse Wills; State Senator Douglas Henry; and one of the authors of this volume, Charles W. Warterfield Jr., who attended the Wallace

University School in 1941, the last year the school was open.

In later years the Alumni Association of the Wallace School was merged with that of Montgomery Bell Academy. When a portrait of Mr. Wallace was commissioned for a new classroom building at MBA named in his honor, some disagreement arose over whether he should be portrayed holding a Bible or Vergil. The portrait shows Wallace holding his Vergil (fig. 1.3).

Nashville was also notably forward looking in providing for the education of females. The Nashville Female Academy was opened in 1816. At the beginning of the Civil War it was the largest school for women in the United States and was one of the first institutions of its kind in the country. In 1860, with a faculty of thirty-eight and an enrollment of 513 pupils, about half of them boarders, the Academy graduated sixty-one students. The school occupied a square of approximately five acres on Church Street, with extensive grounds and several handsome two-story brick buildings. Classes were suspended in 1862 when Federal troops seized the facility for military use. Efforts to reestablish the Academy after the Civil War failed.[17]

St. Cecilia Academy for Young Ladies, founded in 1860, was the only institution for female education that survived the Civil War. It had been founded when Bishop James Whalen, the second bishop of Nashville, requested four Dominican sisters from St. Mary's of the Springs in Columbus, Ohio, to come to Nashville to start a school for young women. A building program was begun in 1861 on the site still in use near the present Metro Center. When Federal troops occupied Nashville in February 1862, St. Cecilia's was the only school in the area permitted to continue holding classes. Authorization was also

1.3 Portrait of Clarence B. Wallace by Louise LeQuire
Courtesy Montgomery Bell Academy.
Photograph: Charles W. Warterfield, Jr.

11

given for the building program, which was already underway, to be completed. Federal sentries watchfully guarded the graduation exercises held in the late spring of 1862, an event attended by large crowds of Nashvillians who were eager for any sort of approved public gathering. The school has held continuous graduations since 1861, is still operated by the Dominicans, and still offers Latin.[18]

Ward Seminary for Young Ladies was founded in 1865 by W. E. Ward, a native of Alabama. The school was non-sectarian, had no ties with any school for boys, and was committed primarily to preparing teachers and to cultivating literary taste and the fine arts. The curriculum was comprehensive. In 1890, Miss Tommie Buchanan, M.A., was listed as the instructor in Latin and Classical History. In the twenty-five year period from 1865 to 1890, the Seminary was attended by more than 3,500 young women. About nine hundred were graduated, and many of them became teachers or achieved other distinction in literature.[19]

Two women from Philadelphia who had been teaching previously in Pulaski, Tennessee, bought Adelicia Acklen's Belmont Mansion in 1889. Their school, known as Belmont Collegiate and Preparatory School, was designed "to establish a high grade school for young ladies, in which they will enjoy, in addition to first-class educational facilities, the advantages and comforts of an elegant home."[20]

Ward Seminary and the Belmont Collegiate and Preparatory School merged in 1913 to form Ward-Belmont, which continued the traditions of both institutions until it closed in 1951. Ward-Belmont was succeeded by Harpeth Hall School for girls. Latin is offered in both the middle and upper schools of Harpeth Hall and may be studied for five years. The Belmont property was bought by the Tennessee Baptist Convention and exists today as Belmont University. Latin is still offered in the curriculum.

Churches and the Classical Languages

Education and religion often came in combination in

early Nashville. The first resident minister in Tennessee of any denomination was Presbyterian. Samuel Doak first came to Tennessee in October of 1777. Doak, like Thomas Craighead, was both fervently religious and well educated. Doak received a classical education from what would later become Washington and Lee University, followed by two years at Princeton. In Tennessee, in addition to building the first Presbyterian churches, he also helped found a number of educational institutions, including Martin Academy (1783), the first educational institution between the Alleghenies and the Mississippi River.[21] Doak's Tusculum Academy, after merger with Greeneville College in the early 1800s, became Tusculum College.

From an early period in America, Presbyterianism maintained high educational standards for its ministers. The synod in 1761, at that time the highest jurisdiction of the denomination, ruled that after students had obtained a college degree, which included intense study of the classical languages, they must then study with some minister for a year in an apprenticeship. Later on in 1792, the General Assembly ruled that the length of apprenticeship must be at least three years.[22]

Such strict educational requirements often were not practical in the frontier lands of Kentucky and Tennessee. With the onset of the Great Revival and the subsequent increased demand for preachers, the requirements were sometimes waived. Some younger clerics in the Cumberland region came up with an expedient to serve the many new congregations: Lower the educational requirements for the ministry. In 1802 the Transylvania Presbytery, which included the Cumberland region, appointed "to the business of exhortation and catechizing" four men who did not have a college education.[23] The following year they were licensed to preach.

Several church leaders, including Thomas Craighead, objected to this licensing, saying the men were "destitute of classical learning, and they [Craighead, et. al.] discovered no extraordinary talents as to justify such measures."[24] One week after the licensing, the Synod of Kentucky in a separate measure, divided the Transylvania Presbytery by forming also the Cumberland Presbytery. The result was two presbyteries that divided Presbyterians into Revival and anti-Revival factions, that is, those who supported waiving of the educational requirements in the classical languages and those who did not.

In addition to lacking classical education, the relatively uneducated candidates also differed doctrinally from mainline Presbyterianism. Reverend Craighead felt that they were not acceptable as clergy and wrote a *fama clamora,* or common fame letter, to the Synod. A common fame letter did not obligate the accuser to assume any responsibility for the charges made. Though the letter appears to be lost, evidence for it is found in the minutes of the Synod of Kentucky on October 22, 1804:

Whereas a Letter having been addressed to [the] Synod containing certain charges and referring to a protest from the Rev. Thomas B. Craighead and others having been taken under consideration and [the] Synod having found it inpractible [sic] regularly to investigate and issue the business at their present Session Ordered therefore that the parties both, the complained of and those being cited, to appear at the next slated Session of Synod with all the light and testimony of the Subject that can be afforded.

The Synod appointed a committee of five to look into the matter and to report at the next meeting. The commission examined the case and in its statement made reference to ". . . it being proclaimed by common fame that the majority of these men are not only illiterate but erroneous in Sentiment."[25] By "illiterate" they meant that the men could not read Latin or Greek.

The commission that was formed as a result of this letter caused the breakup of the Cumberland Presbytery. The Revival or "illiterate" ministers did not recognize the authority of the commission and so did not agree to any of its decisions. Matters grew heated when these "suspect ministers" refused to be examined as candidates for the ministry. Several attempts at reconciliation failed, and on February 4, 1810, at the Dickson County home of Samuel McAdow (one of the "ignorant boys who had been put to sea without chart or compass"), an independent Cumberland Presbytery was constituted. Although this was not at the time intended as a new church or schism, the meeting established the nucleus for the Cumberland Presbyterian Church, the first Protestant denomination to be established in Tennessee.[26]

Roger Williams University and Fisk University— The Classics and the Education of Freed African-Americans

Following the Civil War, Nashville became a center for the education of former slaves with the founding of two major institutions, the Nashville Institute, later Roger Williams University, and Fisk University. The general issue facing education of freed slaves concerned the nature of education that was most desirable for African-Americans in the new era. Edward Wheeler outlines the debate surrounding what form of education was most appropriate:

There was little argument within the ranks of the leading preachers about the need for the freedman to be educated, but there was debate about the type of education that best suited the needs of the freedman. Some believed that the best education for blacks was a classical education, which formed the curriculum offered at most schools and colleges. The classical curriculum was designed to provide an academic education in the liberal arts that prepared students to teach and enter the professions. Extensive training in the classical languages and literature was typical of this type of education.[27]

The contrasting position was that the most desirable education for freedmen would be one that would enable them to serve as independent skilled laborers. Those sharing that point of view eventually established the agricultural and industrial schools and departments.[28] The argument concerning the most appropriate education for African-Americans led eventually to the famous debates between W. E. B. DuBois, the brilliant Fisk graduate and founder of the NAACP, and Booker T. Washington, president of Tuskegee Institute, about the relative merits of classical versus industrial education.[29]

In addition to the two Nashville institutions, Fisk University and Roger Williams University, two other important African-American academies were Tuskegee, founded by Booker T. Washington, and Atlanta University, founded, as was Fisk, by Northern whites of the American Missionary Association. Atlanta University became independent in 1893.

Fisk, Roger Williams University, and Atlanta University promoted a close relationship between religion and education. Initially none had collegiate departments. They started with academic programs limited to grammar school through early high school. By 1886, however, all three had adopted a liberal arts education at the college level with a strong classical basis. Wheeler's study of the school catalogs for 1885-86 reveals the following:

At Roger Williams, students were required to have eight of their first twelve courses in Greek and Latin; six of the ten courses required during the first three years at A.U. centered on Greek and Latin Literature, grammar, history, and culture; and the course offerings at Fisk required nine classes of Greek and Latin combined and two courses each of French and German to go with the eleven non-language courses students took in their first three years.[30]

"It was the opinion of the administrators of these schools," Wheeler concludes, "that a command of the classical languages and literature helped one understand one's own language and disciplined one's mind. Furthermore, the study of Greek was also helpful in the study of the New Testament."[31]

The Nashville Institute was organized in the late 1860s by the American Baptist Home Mission Society for the education of African-Americans. It was rechartered in 1883 as Roger Williams University to honor the great leader of civil and religious liberty, Roger Williams "the best Baptist" Eventually it was situated on Hillsboro Turnpike, two miles from the city limits of Nashville, on the site where Peabody College of Vanderbilt University stands today.

Fisk University was opened in 1867, named for General Clinton B. Fisk, who at that time was head of the Freedman's Bureau. It was first located in a building used as a barracks by Federal troops on Church Street. When the Fisk Jubilee Singers, the choral group that continues in existence to this day, raised their first $20,000 on a fund-raising tour, the money was used to purchase twenty-five acres in North Nashville where Fisk and Meharry Medical College are now located. Fisk was able to survive financially because of the funds raised by the Jubilee Singers on tours between 1871 and 1875.

The catalog of 1871–1872 announced that "privileges are offered alike without distinction of race or sex." By 1906-1907, the catalog added that one of the "environmental advantages of attending Fisk was that "Nashville is the great educational center of the South."[32]

The catalog of 1896-97 states the premises upon which the university was founded:

It has been the unfaltering purpose of the American Missionary Association . . . to make good, in letter and in spirit, this bold and comprehensive promise, made to an emancipated race in the bright morning of its new life.

To found a college and to thoroughly establish among the colored youth the conviction of the absolute necessity of patient, long-continued, exacting, and comprehensive work in preparation for high positions and large responsibilities, seemed fundamental to the accomplishment of the true mission of the university.[33]

The Fisk catalog for that same year indicates that the curriculum was as follows:

Freshman year:
  Fall term: 4 books of Vergil's *Aeneid; Iliad;* algebra
  Winter term: Latin prose composition; *Iliad* 1–3;
    Thucydides; math
  Spring term: Cicero, *De Senectute;* Thucydides; geometry
Sophomore year:
  Fall term: Demosthenes, *On the Crown* (D'Ooge
    edition); calculus; beginning French; rhetoric
  Winter term: Livy (Chase and Stuart); calculus; French;
    civil government
  Spring term: Horace's *Odes* (Chase and Stuart); botany;
    French
Junior year:
  Fall term: Tacitus, *Germania* or *Agricola;* Horace, *Epistles
    and Satires;* physics; German
  Winter term: Sophocles, *Antigone;* German; physiology
  Spring term: Greek literature in translation; German;
    astronomy
Senior year:
  Fall term: psychology; English literature; chemistry
  Winter term: logic; political economy; zoology
  Spring term: ethics; political economy; geology

In 1898 the faculty included Reverend Adam K. Spence, M.A., Dean of the College and Professor of Greek and French; Miss Helen C. Morgan, Professor of Latin; and Miss Clara L. Blake, Instructor in Greek, Latin, and Normal [teaching] Methods. In addition, a theological section of the University offered Hebrew as well as Greek.

Thus at two of Nashville's early universities committed primarily to the education of freed slaves, a classical curriculum was seen as fundamental to all future aspirations. In Nashville, the argument between liberal versus industrial education as the best route to freedom by African-Americans was settled largely in favor of liberal education based on the study of the classics.

Vanderbilt University

Vanderbilt University was founded in 1873, seven years after Fisk University and for related reasons—to help heal the nation of the upheaval wrought by the Civil War and to prepare the survivors for a future that would not be defined by race, in the case of Fisk, or region, in the case of Vanderbilt. Upon the representation of Methodist Bishop Holland McTyeire, Cornelius Vanderbilt gave a munificent endowment for the new university with the hope that it would strengthen the ties "that should exist between all sections of the country."

The first classics professor at Vanderbilt was Milton W. Humphreys, who arrived in Nashville at the invitation of Chancellor Landon C. Garland. Born into a large, rural family in 1844 in what is now West Virginia, Humphreys was largely self-taught as a child and was inspired to a life of learning by the Presbyterian church. After service in the Civil War, he returned to Washington College (later Washington and Lee University) in Virginia where he received inspiration, advice, and loans of money from the president of that institution, Robert E. Lee. After receiving a Ph.D. at the University of Leipzig in 1874 he returned to teach for a year at Washington College. Humphreys chose not to remain at Washington after he was offered a chair in modern languages rather than the classical languages he loved, accepting instead a call to Vanderbilt University as its first professor of Greek. At Vanderbilt he helped design the curriculum, the requirements for admission and graduation, and even the form of the diplomas. Humphreys married the daughter of Chancellor Garland, and in 1883 he was elected president of the American Philological Association, the same year he received the first honorary degree offered by Vanderbilt during the last graduation exercises he supervised.[34]

Other prominent classicists in the early days of Vanderbilt

include the second chancellor of the University, James H. Kirkland, a professor of classics who served as chancellor for forty-four years from 1893 to 1937, and Herbert Cushing Tolman, a classicist of international reputation who taught Greek to Fugitive poet Allen Tate[35] and many others and also served as Dean of the College from 1914 to 1923.

When Vanderbilt's chapter of the national honor society Phi Beta Kappa was established in 1901, with Dean Tolman as the first president, the charter required that a member have had at least one year of either Latin or Greek. To indicate further the classical influences of Phi Beta Kappa, a male chorus sang Horace's Ode 1.22 in Latin at the foundation ceremony.

As late as 1909, entering students at Vanderbilt were supposed to have four years of Latin and three of Greek. For students majoring in English, an additional two years of Latin and Greek were required. After World War I the curriculum became more utilitarian, but undergraduates continued to take classics courses. The *Vanderbilt University Bulletin* for 1921 notes that all students entering Vanderbilt were required to pass entrance examinations in Latin and Greek. The Latin passages were from the works of Vergil or Horace, and the Greek texts were from Xenophon or Homer. Further, it was mandatory that all Arts and Sciences freshmen enroll in English Composition 1A, which required the reading of the *Aeneid* in its entirety and the *Iliad,* from which, if desired, Books 11, 13, 15, and 21 could be omitted. The handbook further stated: "It is recommended by the Faculty that students who intend to take extended work in English or Modern Languages should include in their course both Greek and Latin.[36] Allen Tate recalled that in 1956 T. S. Eliot said to him: "You may not have had a very large curriculum in the Southern colleges, but it was sound, because you had the Latin, Greek and mathematics."[37] Vanderbilt historian Paul K. Conkin notes that when the Fugitives met for reminiscences, those with Vanderbilt degrees emphasized "above all else their classical education"[38] (fig. 1.4).

It was within this strongly-charged classical environment that a remarkable collection of students and faculty were to coalesce. One way or another, all of them were to be influenced by what they were learning as well as by those with whom they were associating.

The Fugitives

Shortly before the beginning of World War I, a group of poets had begun meeting at nine o'clock on alternate Saturday evenings at 3802 Whitland Avenue, where Sidney Mttron Hirsch lived with his brother-in-law, James M. Frank. Hirsch's passion for Greek culture was already well

1.4 Some of the Fugitives at Fugitive Reunion, Vanderbilt University, May 4, 1956. L-R Allen Tate, Merrill Moore, Robert Penn Warren, John Crowe Ransom, Donald Davidson
Photograph: Joe Rudis, courtesy Photographic Archives, Vanderbilt University.

known in Nashville. In May 1913 he had staged a pageant entitled "The Fire Regained" in front of the Parthenon, complete with a cast of six hundred, a huge chorus, and even horses for a chariot race. It is estimated that five thousand people saw the pageant through its six performances.[39]

Other members of the group included Canadian-born Alec B. Stevenson, native Nashvillians William Yandell Elliott and Stanley Johnson, Merrill Moore, William C. Frierson, the cousins Jesse and Ridley Wills, the brothers Milton and Alfred Starr, and Vanderbilt faculty members Walter Clyde Curry and John Crowe Ransom. Ransom, a major influence in the group, had studied Greek and Latin literature and philosophy during his years at Oxford. Early in his career he taught high school Latin. Robert Penn Warren said of Ransom that first of all "he was a classical scholar."[40]

A year after Donald Davidson returned from World War I, he received an appointment as instructor of English at Vanderbilt University, from which he had received his bachelor's degree in absentia in 1917. Davidson joined the group, and in November 1921 he invited a new member, the brilliant young undergraduate Allen Tate. When Robert Penn Warren arrived at Vanderbilt as a freshman in the fall of 1921, he too was invited to join the group. Eventually several of these men were to pursue additional interests in agrarianism, politics, and the state of the South. But in those early years, their passion was for poetry alone: "The pursuit of poetry as an art was the conclusion of the whole matter of living, learning, and being."[41]

This was the group that gave birth to *The Fugitive,* a poetry journal that appeared first in 1922 and continued until December 1925.[42] One of the arguments that was passionately joined was that between Davidson, who argued for a regional poetry, and Tate, who argued for an internationalism based on regionalism. These men were all strongly influenced by the classical education they received at Vanderbilt.

At first Allen Tate may well have placed himself among those for whom the ancient languages were the preserve of the initiated few. In October 1930 Tate contributed to *The New Republic* an essay on "The Bi-Millennium of Vergil," marking the two thousandth anniversary of the Roman poet's birth. Tate notes the paradox of our resorting to translations of Vergil in an age in which the content is irrelevant and only the style is left—unlike, say, the seventeenth century in which the moral appeal of the content might have made translations more appropriate. "For us," writes Tate, "all that is left of Vergil is the special literary exhibit of a great style . . . so that, at a time when Latin is but little read, we need the Latin to get to the beauties of a style."[43]

Two years later Tate revised his views of the significance of the content of the *Aeneid*. Following a picnic with a number of his literary friends at Cassis in Southern France, an event that occasioned the comment that this must be the sort of beach on which Aeneas landed in Italy, Tate bought a copy of the *Aeneid* the next day in Toulon and reread it thoughtfully for several weeks.[44] What followed was an extraordinary literary genesis with identifiable heritage: three major poems and Tate's only novel *The Fathers*, all formed in significant part on Vergilian themes.

All three poems, "The Mediterranean," "Aeneas at Washington," and "Aeneas at New York," employ Vergil's hero as the narrator. "The Mediterranean" poses as its central issue the journey of the poet in search of a tradition. The poem begins with a quotation from Book 3 of the *Aeneid: Quem das finem, rex magne, dolorum*—which means "what end, great king, do you grant to our sufferings?"[45] The third stanza reads:

> *Where we went in the small ship the seaweed*
> *Parted and gave to us the murmuring shore,*
> *And we made feast and in our secret need*
> *Devoured the very plates Aeneas bore.*

In the *Aeneid*, an ill-intentioned harpy imposes a curse determining that although Aeneas and his followers will arrive at their destination, they will suffer such great hunger that they will have to eat their plates. As it happens in the picnic marking their arrival in Italy, Aeneas's son Ascanius notes that the Trojans were eating their pita bread, and he jokes: "Look, we are eating our plates." That moment marks the homecoming that once had seemed too much for Aeneas to hope for. Tate, too, longed for a sense of homecoming into a larger tradition that would help make sense of his own.

The poem ends in Tate's own South, a particular place in the real world—the cornfields and muscadine grapes grow in Tate's native Kentucky—but it is now conceived in universal terms:

> *Westward, westward till the barbarous brine*
> *Whelms us to the tired land where tasseling corn,*
> *Fat beans, grapes sweeter than muscadine*
> *Rot on the vine: in that land were we born.*

In "The Mediterranean," as Radcliffe Squires observes, "Tate for the first time discovered a tradition in which his intellect and sensibility could make a home together."[46] He had discovered the nerve to do the truly creative thing: to take one's actual, lived experience, one's view of the world, one's hopes and despairs, and to appropriate for their purposes a tradition larger than one's own in order to make both experience and tradition a new thing. Call it, if you will, hybrid vigor.

Another of Tate's poems of the same period, "Aeneas at Washington," makes even more explicit connections between the Vergilian literary tradition and Tate's own experience of the world. Here Aeneas is pictured standing in Virginia, gazing across the Potomac at the "city my blood had built." He is recalling how he acted honorably in the fall of Troy, then hoisted his father on his back and set off by sea for the new world,

> *Saving little—a mind imperishable*
> *If time is, a love of past things tenuous*
> *As the hesitation of receding love.*

Aeneas knows that the freight he takes to the New World is slight, but it does contain "a mind imperishable"—if, that is, time is imperishable—and "a love of past things." The past and present, however, the Old World and the New, come together in a peaceful, seemingly timeless collocation, as Tate/Aeneas sees in adjacent lines the fields of Troy and the bluegrass of Kentucky:

> I saw the thirsty dove
> In the lowing fields of Troy, hemp ripening
> And tawny corn, the thickening Blue Grass
> All lying rich forever in the green sun.

Nevertheless, at the end of the poem, Aeneas is, as Tate himself observed later, "a little gloomy." He stands looking at Washington, the first city in the world created for the purpose of government, and wonders what we had built her for.

> Stuck in the wet mire
> Four thousand leagues from the ninth buried city
> I thought of Troy, what we had built her for.

Tate wrote of the poem: "'Aeneas at Washington' seems to ask the reader to think of Aeneas as the founder of Washington as well as of Rome. The westward migration of the Trojans continued across the Atlantic. . . . Aeneas carries his father, on his back out of filial loyalty, and with the egotism which Virgil allows him, he describes himself as a 'true gentleman.' Several friends have pointed out that the description of Troy is more appropriate for parts of Kentucky or Tennessee. Aeneas is a little gloomy. He feels that Washington is not as good as Troy."[47]

Tate's responsiveness to Vergil was due primarily to the latter's own large capacity for conceiving of Rome in political as well as spiritual terms. For all his personal reserve, Vergil was pre-eminently a political poet because he understood Rome's place in history—and that the goals and purposes of individuals may, probably will, be in necessary conflict with those of government. Both, however, are necessary to the civilization and to individuals; the death of either the public or the private realm will ultimately mean the death of both.

Those issues underlie also Tate's novel *The Fathers,* the basic themes of which were conceived as early as 1932, even though the novel was not published until 1938. On the face of it *The Fathers* is a novel of the Civil War. Opening on an April day in 1860 with the funeral of Mrs. Buchan at Pleasant Hill in Virginia, it recounts the destruction of the Buchan family and all its assumptions in the wake of the catastrophe that follows. The literal working of the novel pits Major Buchan, who carries all the burdens of tradition, against his son-in-law George Posey, who knows no tradition at all, the thoroughly modern man. For Allen Tate, however, the literal work of the novel is never separate from the symbolic. According to Arthur Mizener, "The central tension of *The Fathers,* like that of its structure, is a tension between the public and the private life, between the order of civilization, always artificial, imposed by discipline, and at the mercy of its own imperfections, and the disorder of the private life, always sincere, imposed upon by circumstances, and at the mercy of its own impulses."[48] What this means is complex but ultimately simple: The person bound to tradition, represented by Major Buchan, is attractive but can be innocent to the point of moral blindness. The rootless "modern" person, represented in George Posey, can be random and destructive but is not a villain.

What Tate implies in this contrast is that there are two forms of death: the collapse of all individuality into the custom and ritual of formal society, so that a person is caught up in the past and in the views of others; and the collapse of all society into materialistic individualism, so that the social fabric gives way. Put another way, we need traditions to enable us all to live together without being the same. Shared traditions protect individuality, and individuality diversifies and enlivens the shared culture.

If anything can save us from both forms of death, it is tradition rightly understood. Permeating *The Fathers* is a sense of tradition very like that of Vergil's *Aeneid*. The setting of both works, first of all, is civil war—explicit in Tate and, in the *Aeneid*, brooding in its recent consequences. The destruction of the old order, of the Old Troy, is more certain than the shape that the new order will take. In neither world is all the good or evil contained in one side only.

Both history and metaphor can serve to universalize the particularities of our own situation. For Allen Tate, history *was* metaphor. The American Civil War was for Tate what the Trojan War was for Vergil: both a reality and a myth, both a narrative replay of our own past and a touchstone by which to measure our gains and losses. Tate used Vergil and the South as Vergil used Homer and Italy—as analogies by which to comprehend fully the dimensions of our present experience.

Such a process is precarious because it borders perilously close on nostalgia. Nostalgia provokes unease with the present but cannot create positive obligations toward the present or the future. A tremendous courage is required to accept one's past, then to revise it radically for the living of the present.[49] That is the courage of Vergil in the writing of the *Aeneid*. It is the courage also of Allen Tate, who said of himself: "My attempt is to see the present from the past, yet remain immersed in the present and committed to it. I think it is suicide to do anything else."[50]

As early as 1927 Tate wrote to Donald Davidson that Robert Penn Warren, known to his friends as "Red," was "pretty close to being the greatest Fugitive poet. . . . He is the only one of us who has *power*."[51] Part of Warren's power lies in his ability to brace contemporary events with an infrastructure of classical themes in ways that enlarge both. Two of his novels, *Wilderness* (1961) and *A Place to Come To* (1977) demonstrate ways in which Warren brokered this alliance between past and present.

Although Robert Penn Warren wanted to preserve Southern traditions, he also sought to unify the country in a common culture. Toward this apparently paradoxical end he boldly chose the most divisive marker between the regions of the country, the Civil War, as the setting for his novel *Wilderness*. While a symbol of division in this country, the war served also as a source of tradition in both regions, traditions that Warren believed could be revised and enlarged for better purposes through the appropriation of larger traditions still.

The classical themes in *Wilderness* help propose the Civil War as the setting for an American myth or epic. Although Warren does not attempt to write an epic, the characters and, style of *Wilderness* are enhanced with Greek and Roman influences, and the plot features many themes from classical mythology.

Warren believed that people must form myths to find truth in and make sense out of the events in their society, and, as in classical times, these myths should originate from a historical event when people were questioning their ideals and beliefs. This process, said Warren, "must be based on a painfully honest appraisal of society and self in which the whole truth, however difficult it may be to face, is allowed to emerge on its own terms."[52]

Under these conditions, the Civil War qualifies as the best source for such a myth in the United States because, like the Trojan War for the Greeks, it caused conflict and debate in our society during the war. Further, Americans can trace the beginnings of many present debates and political forces to this single event.

Warren's main character in *Wilderness,* Adam, travels to the United States from Europe to fight for the freedom of slaves. During his travels, he begins to understand his life and his interaction with the world around him. While writing in a style similar to epic writers, Warren tells a story that satisfies classical purposes using characters who assume characteristics and actions of mythological figures. *Wilderness* is written in a narrative style that differs from any other novel written by Warren and follows the same epic style used by Homer and Vergil in *The Odyssey* and *The Aeneid*.

Like Odysseus and Aeneas, Adam is on a journey throughout the book. First, Warren describes his trip on a ship from Bavaria and then depicts Adam's trip through the backwoods of Virginia to the site of the battle. During these travels, Adam tries to find meaning in his and other people's actions as Odysseus and Aeneas do. Like the Greeks' destination of Troy in the *Iliad*, his final destination is the Battle of the Wilderness.

Warren's classical themes do not end with the epic genre. Although Adam neither kills his father nor marries his mother, his similarity to Oedipus is easily recognized by his appearance and actions in the plot. Both have a club foot and have a violent fight on a highway over the right-of-way. Both characters see the pain and suffering around them and believe that they are responsible, and because both have accepted this guilt, they appropriate all suffering to themselves. Like Oedipus, Adam finds peace and truth in a grove at the end of the story.

Nor does Adam alone among Warren's characters evoke classical analogies. For example, Maran Goetz Meyerhof clearly represents Demeter, the goddess of the harvest and fertility, by nursing a baby and carrying a basket of grapes,[53] and Jedeen Hawksworth is called "a kind of centaur."[54] Although Hawksworth is not half man and half beast, his appearance represents a modern centaur. His upper body is dressed like a nobleman while his lower body is dressed in old clothes, suggestive of a beast. Finally, Warren describes minor characters with short descriptive phrases such as "the hairy one," "the nondescript man," and "the leaper-over-ferns," much like the Greek epithets in the *Iliad*.[55]

Although *Wilderness* is not one of his most critically acclaimed works, Warren achieves success in creating a "little myth," laying the groundwork for a future American epic set in the Civil War by writing a story rooted with classical themes in a style evocative of epic.[56]

In a later novel, *A Place to Come To* (1977), Warren uses classical themes to underwrite a different kind of tension, that between home and journey, which lies at the heart of Vergil's great Roman epic poem the *Aeneid*. To be on a journey and to be at home are contradictory states. To compose if not reconcile those opposites in *A Place to Come To*, Warren appropriates Vergilian themes as well as references.

His main character Jed Tewksbury leaves Dugton, Alabama, for the University of Chicago and then moves on to Nashville, but not before he has been awkwardly lured in to the world of ideas through Latin literature by his teacher, the limited but good Miss McClatty. "My reading was due to old Miss McClatty," says Jed. "By Christmas of my first year she got me in Caesar; then on past the *Aeneid* to more Virgil, then lots of Horace, Catullus, Tacitus, and Sallust, not to mention lots of Cicero. 'I don't know whatever's come over you, boy,' Miss McClatty would say, and shake her wobbly head. 'It'll make work for me, but I won't stand in your way.'"[57] When Jed wants desperately to make contact with the legendary Dr. Stahlmann at Chicago, he shadows the professor through the streets to his home and finds himself blurting out as his first words the opening lines of the *Aeneid* in Latin.[58]

The Aeneas image continues to inform the novel. Warren opens Part Two with this description of Jed Tewksbury's arrival in Nashville:

When Aeneas came to Carthage, he moved, in a protecting cloud provided by Venus, toward Dido the Queen, whom he was to love, and then, in the fulfillment of his mission, leave her to the fate of the flames. Well, when I came to Nashville, my cloud was a ramshackle bar car, and if my progress was presided over by the Goddess of love, she was embodied in the poor, drunken, courageous female with the clanging charm bracelet and the bum gam. But even if Nashville was scarcely Carthage—only a thriving middle-size commercial city of the Buttermilk Belt—I was to find a queen there.[59]

The importance of the Aeneas theme in this novel transcends the occasional reference or analogy. Jed feels profoundly that he is an exile. A man of few friends, like Aeneas, Jed finally establishes a rich friendship with a refugee scientist with whom the common bond is a sense of homelessness. Nevertheless, the title of the novel betrays its conclusion. Having never returned to Dugton until his mother's death, it is Jed's journey there for her funeral that clarifies for him his sense of place in the world. His final vision is one of returning someday to that place, accompanied by his son Ephraim, to "point out to him all the spots that I had dreamed of pointing out to him." While the filial piety here is directed toward the mother rather than the father, the parent's funeral represents for Jed what it did for Aeneas in Book 5 of the Aeneid—a moment of coalescence between past and future, exile and home, and a rite of passage for the child who represents the next generation—as well as in Book 6, in which Aeneas makes a long, fearful sojourn into the Underworld for a final, momentous meeting with his father.

There were other Fugitive voices than these. Some were less magnanimous, less universal, finally more parochial. For some, classical learning was seen as the preserve for the initiate few, not to be tainted by public appropriation. One of these made known his views concerning the building of the Nashville Parthenon, as we shall see in the Conclusion.

Together, however, these settlers with their dauntless frontier zest, educators with their visions of an Athens in the west for all its people including former slaves, scholarly clergy with their hopes and dreams for the present and future, city leaders with a strong sense of civic responsibility, and Fugitive poets with their universalizing classicism—all these created an environment that nurtured the aspirations of an entire community through their appropriation of a cultural tradition older and broader than their own.

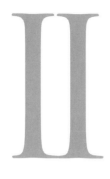

Symbols of a City

Public Architecture in Classical Styles

*All the civilized world acknowledges the existence
of permanent principles established by the wisdom, strength
and beauty of the proportions and symmetry of the Grecian Temples.*

WILLIAM STRICKLAND
The Three Orders, 1848

A merican civic architecture began with a gentleman sitting on a bench in the French city of Nimes. He sat there in 1787, gazing whole hours at the Maison Carrée, "like a lover at his mistress," in his own account." The man was Thomas Jefferson and the object of his desire was a Roman temple constructed in 16 B.C. In a letter to the Comtesse de Tessé, the aunt of Lafayette, Jefferson describes it as "the most perfect remains of antiquity which exist on earth" (fig. 2.1). Jefferson felt rapture for more than the best-preserved Roman temple in existence. The building in Nimes presented to his mind's eye an entire culture. "The city of Rome is actually existing in all the splendor of its empire," he wrote to the Comtesse.[1]

For a citizen of the Enlightenment, with dreams of a new republican experiment on the other side of the Atlantic, the Maison Carrée spoke a language Jefferson could understand and use. It was a language he had read in books, such as his set of the works of Palladio, but never before had Jefferson seen it expressed so perfectly.

It is a long way from Nimes to Nashville, but the capital of Tennessee has had a love affair with the classical style no less devoted than that of Thomas Jefferson. Through two

32

centuries of progress and change, Nashville's predilection for the classical has remained, surviving cyclical shifts such as the romanticism of the late nineteenth century, the eclecticism of the early twentieth century, the modernist challenge of the mid-twentieth century, and the confusion of styles prevalent in the late twentieth century. The perennial appeal of Greek and Roman architecture has resulted in buildings of monumental and successful interpretation, as well as structures of lesser distinction, but Nashville's public image remains defined by classical architecture.

Establishing an Architectural Identity

After the Revolutionary War, with the political structure and instruments of a new government at least tenuously in place, the American republic was faced with a challenge and an opportunity unique in history: the selection of an architectural imagery or style to embody, symbolize, and house a new government.

Prior to the Revolution, all significant buildings constructed by the colonists reflected national origins in Europe, with the House of Burgesses and other structures in Williamsburg, Virginia, representing the most architecturally significant effort by the English to project a presence in their

2.1 Maison Carrée, Nîmes, France
Library of Congress

33

North American empire. Buildings of many styles—Dutch, Georgian, Tudor, even Spanish—had been built along the eastern seaboard, but all were inadvertent symbols of the very European monarchies, empires, and cultures against which the Revolution was directed. It was clear that the new nation required its own architecture.[2]

The quest to achieve this goal focused on the overriding needs of the new country: reason, order, stability, and unity. President George Washington first spoke of an architecture of unity in his inaugural address when he envisioned "a grand Columbian Federal city" to symbolize the nation's authority. His statement began years of discussion among Washington, Thomas Jefferson, and James Madison regarding the nation's capitol and the buildings within it.[3]

Washington's vision and leadership were shared by Thomas Jefferson, who brought to the discussions not only a passion for architecture, but also a broad knowledge of the classical styles, both Greek and Roman. He had already designed the Virginia State Capitol (fig. 2.2) in 1789, when the debate between proponents of a wholly new federal city and the advocates for anointing an existing city with the designation of capital was engaged. Inspired by his beloved Maison Carrée, Jefferson's Virginia Capitol demonstrated the

2.2 Virginia State Capitol, Richmond
Photograph: James A. Hoobler

suitability of classical design as a symbol of governmental authority. Jefferson thus became the first American leader to envision a plan for housing a new government in the forms of ancient architecture.[4]

The concept of a wholly new capital city triumphed for many of the same reasons that the classical became the style of choice for its buildings. For a new government, a symbolically weighted place went hand-in-hand with a symbolically weighted style.

The District of Columbia was located by George Washington on the border between Maryland and Virginia to appease rival factions in North and South. The planning of the new city, with suggestions from Washington and Jefferson, was commissioned from Major Pierre Charles L'Enfant, a French architect and military engineer who had served as an aide to Washington during the war. As he surveyed the site in 1791, L'Enfant fixed on the two highest ridges for the two centers of government: the house of the executive and the house of Congress. From this symbolic division L'Enfant radiated a dynamic web of diagonals overlaid by a rational grid of streets. Within this framework, L'Enfant envisioned a series of buildings styled to convey the same message as the plan: a government aggressively radiating into the future yet grounded with stable roots in the past.[5]

Throughout the formative years of the architecture of government, the founders and their architects associated the logical purity and form of Greek architecture with democracy in Greek city-states, whereas they connected the Roman style with a powerful centralized authority in an expanding empire. These key characteristics of ancient systems of government were thought to be compatible with the new American republic, and, as a result, the early shapers of the nation adopted a classical architecture symbolizing Greek democratic ideals and Roman strengths. As the young government grew into the space provided in L'Efant's plan, excellent examples of classical building styles were constructed, and it became apparent to the founders that such an architecture

35

was eminently suitable to the ideological persuasion of the new nation and the projection of its authority.

The symbolic value of the classical style was further demonstrated in the design of buildings to house the banking system of the country, a system that had been particularly difficult to organize. Although the architecture of the earliest banks had been generically classical in form, the Second Bank of the United States in Philadelphia (fig. 2.3), built in 1817 in a stern Doric style, emphasized the qualities of dignity, reliability, and stability so badly needed in an era of financial turmoil. This handsome building was an early indication of the talents of its designer, William Strickland, who would spend his last years in Nashville establishing the architectural basis for the city's appellation as the "Athens of the South."[6]

Classical Stirrings: Nashville to the 1840s

Because of its remote location on the frontier across the mountains, the Nashvillians of the eighteenth century did not have access to, or knowledge of, the classical design philosophy emerging in the major cities of the eastern seaboard, nor to the artisans and architects located there. Thus the earliest public buildings were modest, utilitarian structures largely devoid of a recognizable architectural style beyond that of the purely vernacular.

In the early decades of the nineteenth century, however, Nashville enjoyed a prosperity and stability following treaties with the Native Americans in the region that allowed the city's development as the center of trade and transportation on the Cumberland River. The result was a need and desire for buildings of greater size and sophistication. Knowledgeable builders such as Nathan Vaught, Joseph Reiff, and William Hume were attracted to the area, and they came equipped with an appreciation for the architectural trends prevalent in the east as well as in the newly available builders' guides and handbooks. These publications provided guidelines for the use of classical details freely adapted and combined with elements of the older Federal style.[7] The result was a number of early nineteenth-century public buildings of considerable interest. Among these were the Nashville Inn (fig. 2.4), the Bank of the United States of 1827,[8] and the Davidson County Courthouse of 1829 (fig. 2.5). A modest three-story building with pilasters and pediment as well as a stylized cupola, the courthouse was, in all probability, the earliest classically influenced structure in Nashville.

Practicing architects were not present in Nashville until Hugh Roland opened his office in 1818. During the 1820s

2.3 Second Bank of the United States, Philadelphia

Photograph: Nicholas Gianopolous

and 1830s the distinction between carpenters, builders, and architects was unclear, because no formal degree or license was required for the title of "architect." In addition, all three professions relied, to some extent, on published guidelines in adapting the forms, motifs, and details of tradition to current building needs. If a distinction can be made, it is through the sophistication of the sources used. Palladio's edition of Vitruvius (1556) and his own *Il Quattro libri dell' architettura* (1570), Vignola's *Regole delle cinque ordini* (1562), and Stuart and Revett's *Antiquities of Athens* (1762-1794) were the most historically and architecturally significant.

In Nashville during this period, the title "architect" was

2.4 *Nashville Inn*
Tennessee Historical Society
Collection, Tennessee State
Library and Archives

2.5 *Davidson County Courthouse, 1829*
Tennessee Historical Society
Collection, Tennessee State
Library and Archives

ascribed to professionals such as James M. Hughes, Mason Vannoy, and the prolific David Morrison, all of whom utilized classical elements. Vannoy's Presbyterian Church of 1832 (fig. 2.6) and Morrison's McKendree Methodist Church of 1833 (fig. 2.7) demonstrate an increasing sophistication in classical design. The Presbyterian Church featured an excellent Doric portico. The Methodist building was entered through a modest Doric two-columned recessed portico.[9]

Morrison's Methodist Church was surmounted by a "monopteron," an architectural element from Greek antiquity of cylindrical form surrounded by a single row of columns, which was similar to those atop his Courthouse and Penitentiary. The employment of this simple classical element as a means to identify civic buildings was a pale reflection of the grander Roman-inspired domes that were growing in popularity as symbols of governmental authority in the eastern states.[10] Unfortunately, none of the above buildings remains. Morrison's most important monopteron,

2.6 First Presbyterian Church, 1832

2.7 McKendree Methodist Church

Tennessee Historical Society Collection, Tennessee State Library and Archives

however, the Doric "tempietto"[11] that was designed as the funerary monument of Andrew and Rachel Jackson, still stands in The Hermitage garden (fig. 2.8). In combination with the house's monumental portico of Corinthian columns, this monopteron is a fitting memorial to Nashville's first important patron of classical architecture.

Classical Nashville Comes of Age: The Tennessee State Capitol

When the architect William Strickland arrived in Nashville in 1843, he must have thought he had come to the edge of the wilderness. The most notable of the city's buildings were gathered near the public square with its open-air market: the Courthouse, the City Hotel, the Bank of the United States, and the Nashville Inn, where the architect was to make his home for the remaining years of his life. Beyond the square, Nashville quickly lapsed into a town of low-rise wood and brick structures punctuated by the spires

2.8 Andrew Jackson tomb and monument

Photograph: Charles W. Warterfield, Jr.

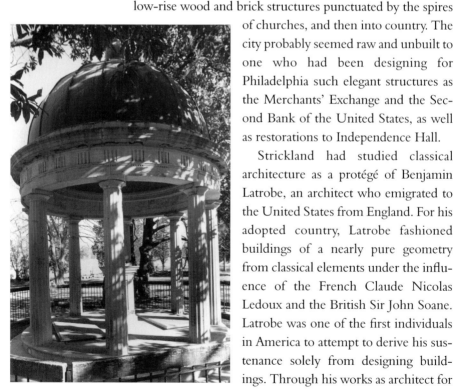

of churches, and then into country. The city probably seemed raw and unbuilt to one who had been designing for Philadelphia such elegant structures as the Merchants' Exchange and the Second Bank of the United States, as well as restorations to Independence Hall.

Strickland had studied classical architecture as a protégé of Benjamin Latrobe, an architect who emigrated to the United States from England. For his adopted country, Latrobe fashioned buildings of a nearly pure geometry from classical elements under the influence of the French Claude Nicolas Ledoux and the British Sir John Soane. Latrobe was one of the first individuals in America to attempt to derive his sustenance solely from designing buildings. Through his works as architect for buildings during Jefferson's administration, as well as such works as his Bank of Pennsylvania in Philadelphia and his Baltimore Cathedral, and through the influence of his students—Strickland and Robert Mills among them—Latrobe established the American architect as a professional.

Because of Latrobe's tutelage, Strickland was thoroughly familiar not only with the application of classical design but also with its symbolic value. His commission to design the Tennessee State Capitol of 1845 was a dramatic gesture of confidence on the part of Tennesseans and represents the first westward projection of the classical style for the architecture of government.[12]

This confidence was the result of steady economic growth and the political importance that Andrew Jackson's Presidency signalled for the region. The Nashville that Strickland found upon his arrival was a city in which pioneers had become settlers. In spite of periods of political and financial instability, the city had developed quickly, with the public arena and the great houses of the surrounding plantations vying for pride of place.

The region's economy was based on agriculture, with Nashville, as the center of commerce and trading, serving the surrounding farms and the numerous large plantations. This economy, in conjunction with staunchly democratic regional attitudes based on precedents in classical political and economic theories, assured the successful adoption of Greek classicism in the architecture of public buildings. The new classical structures articulated in three dimensions the notion that the people of the region were themselves heirs to Greek culture.

The presence in Nashville of an architect of Strickland's training and reputation was both a catalyst to higher architectural quality and an indication of Tennessee's determination to call attention to the state's importance. The Capitol that Strickland designed furthered both purposes.

The building's basic temple form (fig. 2.9) instantly transformed the highest hill in the town's center into Nashville's acropolis. Set on a high base in the manner of Roman religious buildings, the Capitol is determinedly Greek in its exterior detailing. Strickland's design, however, manipulates ancient example by the logic of current practical and symbolic needs. The columned porticoes, placed democratically on four sides, constrict the peristyle—the range of columns typically surrounding all four walls of the Greek temple—to the building's actual entrances. The entrances allude to the porches of the Erechtheion on the Athenian Acropolis while signalling how the structure actually works.

The architect's selection of the Ionic rather than the Doric order for the columns' capitals was assuredly a self-conscious one, for Strickland had already demonstrated in Philadelphia his mastery of all the Greek orders. The choice

2.9 Tennessee State Capitol, 1845

Photograph: Charles W. Warterfield, Jr.

resulted in a style of sophisticated elaboration applied to forms of massive simplicity. On the Attic peninsula the Ionic order had succeeded the Doric in supremacy much as Tennessee was succeeding the east in the evolution of a national architecture.

Avoiding the Roman dome so prevalent in capitols past and future, Strickland topped his temple with an adaptation of the Choragic Monument of Lysicrates,[13] an ancient artifact in the Corinthian order that he had already used with success on the Merchants' Exchange (fig. 2.10). The monumental scale and strength of character in the relation of base to temple to top—overlaid with a filigree of intensely worked detail—makes the building even today one of the country's outstanding examples of Greek Revival architecture.[14]

Inside, Strickland again adapted precedent to symbolic and practical requirements. The entrance level, containing the administrative offices of government, arches firmly from

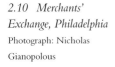

2.10 Merchants'
Exchange, Philadelphia
Photograph: Nicholas
Gianopolous

the temple's solid base by means of groin vaults that visually and structurally balance horizontal and vertical thrusts (fig. 2.11). The halls that bisect this level are weighty and portentous, almost dim in ambience. This is architecture of purpose, housing the executive and constitutional officers who make the State of Tennessee work.

A grand interior staircase establishes a processional path upwards from dimness into light. A hall (fig. 2.12) defined by Roman arches which support the cupola soars forty-two feet, leading to the chambers of the House and Senate. The monumental space establishes the primacy of government by representation; its massive windows shed the clarity of the Enlightenment onto this government's machinery.

The interiors are marked by the same creative tension between stern, simple structure and elaborate detailing that Strickland had already established on the exterior. Walls of plain Tennessee limestone, laid vertically to utilize its whorls and graining as the only decoration, form a severe contrast to painted ceilings and highly worked chandeliers and oak doors. In effect, Strickland was pushing the outer limits of Greek style and Roman construction across the Appalachians, extending the premises of the classical style as the country was extending its grasp of the new land to the southwest.

Classical Maturity Beyond the Capitol

The dominant position of Capitol Hill almost necessitated that the influence of William Strickland would reach beyond its crest. The Capitol-in-progress led most immediately to a request for the exercise of his design skills on the tomb of President James Polk, which now stands on the northeast flank of the Hill. Beyond its slopes, Strickland received commissions for several other Nashville buildings, among them the First (now Downtown) Presbyterian Church. It is widely, if erroneously, believed that in 1846 he designed the Second Presbyterian Church, which no longer stands. There is, however, no documentation for this ascription. It was more probably the work of James M. Hughes.[15]

*2.11 (above) Tennessee
State Capitol, Supreme
Court room*

*2.12 Tennessee State
Capitol, main hall*

Photographs: Charles W.
Warterfield, Jr.

2.13 Bank of Nashville, 1853

Tennessee Historical Society Collection, Tennessee State Library and Archives

2.14 Union Bank of Tennessee, 1853

James A. Hoobler Collection, Tennessee State Library and Archives

In 1853 two bank buildings were designed in the Greek temple form that followed the successful example that Strickland had set earlier in Philadelphia. These were the small Bank of Nashville by James M. Hughes (fig. 2.13) and the Union Bank of Tennessee by Francis Strickland, William's son (fig. 2.14). Although the Union Bank was a successful exercise in the Greek style, Francis Strickland's subsequent Davidson County Courthouse of 1855 (fig. 2.15) lacked the purity and conviction of his father's Capitol, in spite of the close resemblance between the two. The son's weaknesses are most evident in the awkward proportions of the Corinthian columns and the absence of a basement story at ground level.

Also evident in the Courthouse design—especially in the decidedly unclassical Italianate brackets in the frieze and in the odd panelled parapet at the side portico—was an emerging public taste for a mixture of classical prototypes with other newly fashionable historical styles. This appetite directed the course of architecture away from the classical path for four decades.[16] Nor was the Davidson County Courthouse the only harbinger of an architectural weather change. The token Corinthian entrance on the massive Italianate block of the Maxwell House Hotel was only a slight

*2.15 Davidson County
Courthouse, 1855*
James A. Hoobler Collection,
Tennessee State Library and
Archives

gesture of respect to the classical style. The Maxwell House was destroyed by fire in 1961.

Although Adolphus Heiman was a contemporary of William Strickland's, Heiman's architectural career exemplifies the eclecticism then coming into fashion. A Prussian with a knowledge of the architecture of New York and New Orleans as well as Europe, Heiman came to the art of building as a stonecutter. His work shows a less fervent commitment to classical forms than that of Strickland, in spite of the fact that he arrived in Nashville in 1837 with a sixteenth-century copy of Vignola under his arm. Like so many nineteenth-century architects, Heiman embraced in his career several styles, Gothic and Italianate as well as classical. That he nevertheless had a firm grasp of the language of classicism is demonstrated by such Nashville structures as St. Mary's Catholic Church (Fifth Avenue, North, and originally the Cathedral) of 1845 and the Medical Department of the University of Nashville in the 1850s.

Heiman's design for St. Mary's (fig. 2.16), which has been substantially altered in several remodellings, is both dignified and restrained. A basic temple form is highlighted by a recessed portico with Ionic columns and pediment, as well as a domed belfry in the Corinthian order. In its original open form, this feature was reminiscent of the monoptera already in evidence in several Nashville structures. Its resemblance to the State Capitol cupola created the erroneous belief that the church was designed by Strickland.

The most purely Grecian of Heiman's buildings was the no-longer-standing Medical Department of the University of Nashville (fig. 2.17). Its entrance featured the Ionic order, whose upper part (the entablature, consisting of architrave, frieze, and cornice) surrounded the building, while the piers slightly projecting from the walls (or pilasters) and pedimented gables serve as strong allusions to the peripteral columns and pediments of the Greek temple. After the Capitol, it was the most imposing Greek Revival building in Nashville.

Heiman's design for the Adelphi Theater (fig. 2.18) was a departure from the Grecian and demonstrates a predilection for a classical style filtered through Renaissance precedent. The facade was dominated by a monumental arched entry flanked by simplified pilasters, all set within and against a plain, unadorned parapet. The projecting "Roman triumphal

2.16 St. Mary's Catholic Church, 1845
Photograph: Charles W. Warterfield, Jr.

arch" and side porches break the smooth planes of the walls found in the Medical Department and demonstrate that Heiman looked at the classical style through eclectic eyes. Substantially remodelled in the early twentieth century, the theater was razed in 1953.

Adolphus Heiman did not share Strickland's certitude that the proportions of the Greek temple were "permanent principles." For Heiman the classical style was not a matter of permanent principles but rather a matter of choice. The grip that classicism had exercised on Nashville's architectural imagination was weakening.

2.17 Medical Department of the University of Nashville, ca. 1850
Tennessee State Library and Archives

2.18 Adelphi Theater
Photograph: T. M. Schlier, collection of Herbert Peck

The decade of 1845 to 1855 was, nevertheless, a "golden age" of classical architecture. It was characterized by the optimism and idealism of the "era of manifest destiny," a destiny manifested in an architecture of classical principles, tastes, and choices. In 1855 a comparison of Nashville with ancient Athens was not only possible, but popular. The temple of state government on Nashville's highest hill demonstrated the city's good fortunes in the same way that the ancient monuments on the Acropolis reflected those of classical Athens.

The Unclassical Interlude

The Civil War proved to the citizens who lived through it what such architects as Adolphus Heiman had already suspected: that a new architectural language was needed for the buildings of public life. For the winners, the war had triumphantly settled the definition of the nation's southern boundaries and what kind of life was appropriate within them. Aspects of nationhood other than the rational expansion of enlightenment into a wilderness now required expression. Stability and permanence were no longer appropriate, even possible, metaphors for a country hurtling west on rails of iron.

The losers wandered home through the empty shells of market towns. They gazed across war-torn fields to columns whose toppled and broken state now mocked the agrarian ideals these props of Southern nationalism had symbolized. Stability and permanence were ashes in the mouths of those wondering how they were to eat.

By virtue of its early and easy conquest and long occupation by Federal forces, Confederate Nashville was not destroyed for its sympathies. But in the aftermath of war, Nashville's image of itself had changed. The city that had sent Andrew Jackson off to Washington was not the place from which Andrew Johnson departed for the White House. The Nashville that pulled itself together and went on with the business of living placed its faith and its symbols not in government but in commerce. The government buildings erected in the city—the U.S. Customs House, for example—housed the commercial functions of government. And a world in which commerce is king needed an architecture to express its progress and repress its problems, an architecture different from that required by Jacksonian democracy.

During the latter half of the nineteenth century, public architecture in Nashville and all over the newly reunited United States became a kaleidoscope of styles.[17] Sentimental references to the Greek Revival never entirely disappeared from the South, but the stable architectural imagery of the 1840s was a truly lost cause. And the South that had grimly decided to rise again was determined to do so in an architectural dress that would not distinguish the region from its Northern counterpart.

While most of the postwar styles had vague historical allusions—Second Empire to the French Renaissance, Richardsonian Romanesque to pre-Renaissance Europe—the ideology that they sprang from is better characterized as organic. The Industrial Revolution was growing, and architecture was trying to keep pace. Precedent and principle had been important in prewar theory; they counted for little in the brave new world that followed the conflict. Buildings were needed for the businesses of educating, preaching, healing, and money-making. Those buildings—such as the now-razed structures on Seventh Avenue—were everything that classicism was not (fig. 2.19). They sported the irregular profiles and elaborate textures that appear in nature and that we characterize architecturally as Victorian. The Nashville skyline was defined by spires and steeples, towers and turrets, instead of columns and cupolas. Onion domes, sunburst moldings, ocular windows, and vegetative patterns of stained glass may in hindsight be viewed as abstractions from a natural world the nation no longer feared, but dominated with increasing confidence. They are also expressions of what money could buy right from the machine shop. In the period that saw wealth arising not from the products of land but from the commerce of industrialism, conspicuous consumption of architectural elements was the ultimate expression of consumer self-confidence.

It was only with the United States Centennial of 1876 that the country paused to catch its breath. Citizens gathered around Philadelphia's Independence Hall and found in their collective roots a classically-inspired architecture worthy of reviving as a tribute to how far the nation had come since 1776.

Classicism in Control: 1897–1925

The American people have seen "The Classics" for the first time . . .
I can see all America constructed in noble, dignified classical style.
DANIEL BURNHAM
Architectural Director of the Columbian Exposition, 1893

It took Nashville two decades before the spirit of the U. S. Centennial had a significant impact on public building. If the classicism of mid-century was characterized by a grace worthy of Chopin, the classicism of the 1890s marched into town with all the pomp and patriotism of John Philip Sousa. Although buildings of various styles were included in Tennessee's Centennial Exposition (fig. 2.20), discussed more fully in Chapter 4, a fresh view of classical styles dominated the exposition in much the same way that it would dominate American architecture for over three decades.

When the Tennessee Centennial Exposition opened on May 1, 1897, a Parthenon and a pyramid stood outlined in electric lights above a man-made lake teeming with gondolas. The Streets of Cairo vied with the Chinese village for public attention on a site that little more than a century ago had been a wilderness. The state was about to enter what would later be called the American Century, and it felt free to pick and choose from history and geography in expressing its self-confident mastery of time and place.

In the wake of the U.S. Centennial, anniversary exposi-

53

tions celebrating technological and commercial advances spread westward, mimicking the original patterns of settlement. Chicago's Columbian Exposition of 1893 anointed Beaux-Arts classicism as the chosen style for the elaborate complexes of exhibit halls and monuments that these expositions required. The temporary White City inaugurated

*2.19 Vine Street
Christian Church and
The Temple, 1880s*
Photograph: Charles W.
Warterfield, Jr.

*2.20 Tennessee
Centennial Exposition,
1897*
Library of Congress

American urban planning and became the model for the City Beautiful Movement, which fostered the development of permanent complexes of cultural and government buildings for the enlightenment of public life.[18]

The Parisian school known as the École des Beaux-Arts taught that a disciplined rationality could be achieved in the planning of cities through a system of primary and subordinate avenues lined with buildings in a classical imperial style. The movement brought architecture into the academy, and many American architects were in attendance. On their return from abroad, or from American schools influenced by Beaux-Arts theory, these architects found a national economy that, after 1885, was also characterized by the exercise of a controlling discipline, in this case to maximize profit. This was the age of the great conglomerates, the trusts of railroads, steel, electricity, oil, money and securities, even labor, that consolidated the means of production into massive mechanisms. It was also an age in which our culture was marked by Jim Crow laws validated by Plessy vs. Ferguson, by imperial wars in Cuba and the Philippines, and by anxiety aroused by new waves of immigration.

The search for order in a culture becoming increasingly more complex needed an architecture to follow suit, and classicism was ideally suited for this purpose. The style returned to center stage as the best way to symbolize the grandeur, prosperity, and power of the now-mature republic, the best way to discipline the rampant individualism of the cities.

It is ironic that a revival of classicism was embraced at a time when the technologies of steel frame construction and the elevator made possible structures of a distinctly unclassical verticality and non-human scale. Architects going back to Alfred B. Mullett, supervising architect for the U.S. Treasury Department after 1866, and William A. Potter, the designer of Nashville's Gothic-style Customs House, had in the nineteenth century apprehended flaws in applying classicism to all civic architecture. They felt that the style was often irrelevant in its disregard for contemporary needs and issues.[19]

There were many twentieth-century architects who agreed, but the urge to build higher and bigger was tempered by a search for order that sought to express more clearly the structural and functional realities of the building. Clarity and harmony were in some cases achieved through a uniquely personal idiom, such as those developed by Louis Sullivan and Frank Lloyd Wright. It was more common, however, to return to classical principles of design and often to a re-use of classical forms of ornament. The public's appetite for Grecian orders and Roman planning reflected a will that the country march into the new century in a dignified and stately manner, perhaps because beneath the surface of self-confidence lay an unease about just where the country was rushing at such speed.

In Nashville the compromise between old and new, stability and progress, is typified by the Stahlman Building (fig. 2.21). Designed by Otto Eggers of New York with Carpenter & Blair of Nashville in 1905, Nashville's first high-rise office building employed a steel frame and elevators, but these modernities were discreetly concealed within an envelope that features a Doric portico and a stylized neoclassical cornice, the latter of which has been removed. The Stahlman Building is one example of what kinds of buildings Nashville needed during the prosperous years at the turn-of-the-century. No significant new government structures were added to the city's architectural horizon, but office, educational, and religious buildings, as well as lodges, hotels, and monuments in classical styles steered a course away from the architectural individualism of the later nineteenth century.

Nashville's architects were well versed in the application of a variety of styles and made free and eclectic use of them in the design of residences during the first quarter of the century. In public and institutional buildings, however, the styles of choice were the neoclassic and the Beaux-Arts classic. The neoclassic is characterized by buildings of an otherwise simple form on which classical details and orders are

56

well-articulated. In distinction, Beaux-Arts compositions are larger, more grandiose, even ostentatious, with colossal orders and a highly enriched ornamentation.

The campus plan of George Peabody College (fig. 2.22) is Nashville's most significant example of classical Roman planning. Ludlow & Peabody Architects of New York went back to Thomas Jefferson's plan for the University of Virginia to symbolize the rational enlightenment that the teachers' college was intended to effect in its students and in their

2.21 Stahlman Building, 1905
Photograph: Charles W. Warterfield, Jr.

students in turn. The hierarchical layout of the whole campus reflects the Beaux-Arts influence: the subordinate yards intersect the primary quardrangle, and the domed Social Religious Building (fig. 2.23), the 1915 structure also by Ludlow & Peabody and extensively renovated in the mid-1990s, crowns the gradually rising site. The campus articulates in three dimensions the disciplined homogeneity that education was supposed to foster among the citizenry.[20]

The straightforward and symmetrical arrangement of individual buildings on the campus, all compatible interpretations of a primarily Roman style, reveals the Beaux-Arts predilection for the colossal colonnade and enriched detailing. Although several architects were at work on the Peabody campus, there is a remarkable harmony among their buildings, the details of which form a veritable encyclopedia of classical architecture. And the architecture mirrors an educational system meant to standardize the cultural mission of its graduates. Here, too, variety gives way to harmony.

Several of Nashville's domed buildings respond, on a more modest scale, to the example set by the Social Religious Building at Peabody. The Woodland Presbyterian Church of 1917 (fig. 2.24) is significant because of the prominent dome of its roof, as is the City Market of 1922 (fig. 2.25). Designed by Henry C. Hibbs, the market's oth-

2.22 George Peabody College campus
Vanderbilt University Department of Campus Planning

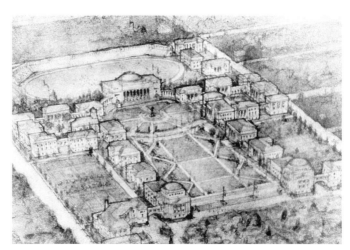

2.23   Social-Religious Building, Peabody campus, 1915

2.24   Woodland Presbyterian Church, 1917

2.25   City Market, 1922

Photographs: Charles W. Warterfield, Jr.

erwise simple forms are given civic status by the classical entrance portico and well-proportioned dome over the central structure. A historically appealing detail is the small monopteron atop the dome—an echo of those that adorned the earliest civic buildings on Nashville's public square.

Belmont Methodist Church (fig. 2.26) was completed in 1927 to the design of architect George Waller. The restraint and purity of its Ionic portico represent a neoclassicism executed by one of the last of Nashville's architects with a thorough grasp of the ethos of the Grecian style. Waller's confident assimilation of classicism can also be seen in the facade of Cavert School, done in 1928 (fig. 2.27). The prominence of its entrance porch and the richness of its details transform the little red school house of popular myth into a Beaux-Arts monument to a classical education.

The highly encrusted classical ornamentation characterizing the Beaux-Arts style are nowhere more evident in Nashville than in the Hermitage Hotel (fig. 2.28) and the Doctors' Building on Church Street (fig. 2.29). Both buildings illustrate the increasingly popular use of polychrome terra cotta adapted to classical detail and ornament, a revival of ancient southern Italic practice. Designed by École graduate J. Edwin Carpenter in 1910, the Hermitage Hotel is the Beaux-Arts version of the Italian Renaissance palazzo. Its lavish facade (now missing much of its original ornament) and public interiors were intended to attract customers by suggesting that the accommodations were princely enough for a modern-day Medici. Another 1910 structure, Edward E. Dougherty's Doctors' Building utilizes an elaborate balustraded cornice punctuated with classical urns to confer a princely status upon the practitioners of the art of healing.

If an elaborately worked ornamentation is one face of Beaux-Arts classicism, another is the style's grand scale and monumentality. A 1913 creation by architects Gardner and Seal, the basic block form of the Frost Building (Southern Baptist Sunday School Board) (fig. 2.30) is almost overpowered by its colossal Roman Corinthian columns, pilasters,

2.26 (above) Belmont Methodist Church, 1927

2.27 Cavert School, 1928

Photographs: Charles W. Warterfield, Jr.

61

and entablature. The Masonic Grand Lodge (fig. 2.31), designed in 1925 by Asmus & Clark, is another large simple mass, this time a cube, faced with a colossal order. The engaged Ionic columns, pilaster, and cornice, set above a massive base and topped with a curious roof structure, itself in the form of a Greek temple, demonstrate the ability of the Beaux-Arts architects of the period to employ classicism in innovative ways.

Although smaller than the neighboring Stahlman Building, the American National Bank (now American Trust) Building (fig. 2.32) was in its original form a self-confident temple to the goals of commerce. Designed in 1926 by Henry C. Hibbs, the highly-embellished Roman Ionic order and bold pediment, complete with classical ornaments at apex and ends (acroteria), demonstrate a conviction not found in the fast-approaching Depression years.

The War Memorial Building on Legislative Plaza is perhaps the best summary statement of classicism in pre-Depression Nashville. A tribute to the dead of World War I,

2.28 Hermitage Hotel, 1910

Photograph: Charles W. Warterfield, Jr.

it is also a memorial to the classical spirit itself. The War Memorial, and the other Beaux-Arts structures of the period, are the last in Nashville to reflect a confident identification with the ancient world. A building of 1925 by Edward E. Dougherty (fig. 2.33), the Memorial's severe Doric colonnade and portico, approached by a monumental series of steps, recall the entrance through the Propylaeon to the Athenian Acropolis.

Standing in the open courtyard beyond (fig. 2.34), a bronze youth holds in his hand a Nike, the Greek symbol for victory. His sandaled foot rests on a ship's prow. The heavy-jawed face and stylized musculature of the almost-nude figure—classical precedent modified by New World standards of seemliness—recall the heroic style of archaic sculpture, a reference reinforced by the surrounding roll call of the dead. The legend reads, "In Memory of the Sons of Tennessee who gave their lives in the Great War, 1914–1918." The glory and the public spirit of classical Greece were now ours.

The Depression of Classicism

The dark days of the Depression called into question the viability of the economic system and the republican form of

2.29 Doctors' Building, 1910

Photograph: Charles W. Warterfield, Jr.

2.30 Frost Building (Baptist Sunday School Board), 1913   Photograph: Charles W. Warterfield, Jr.

government of the United States. Some people became interested in socialism or in other utopian "isms" imported from somewhere else as answers to the question: "Buddy, can you spare a dime?" Not surprisingly, the 1930s also saw a challenge to the classical architecture that had served as such an effective symbol of American capitalism and democracy.

As early as the 1920s, an import from abroad known generically as modernism had gradually begun to eclipse the popularity of classicism. Ironically, the machine-age aesthetic sprang from many of the same motives that had in the past produced a classical revival. *The International Style: Architecture Since 1922,* the publication that accompanied the 1931 exhibition on the subject at the Museum of Modern Art in New York City, is an iron-fisted statement on the why's of modernism. In the preface, museum director Alfred H. Barr writes that "some of us who have been *appalled by this chaos* [italics added] turn with the utmost interest and expectancy to the International Style. . . . The Style requires discipline and restraint, the will to perfect as well as the will to invent. And this is contrary to the American cult of individualism."[21] In the past we had turned from chaos to columns and capitals.

The triumph of the International Style was gradual

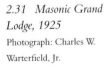

2.31 Masonic Grand Lodge, 1925
Photograph: Charles W. Warterfield, Jr.

because practitioners of the architecture of classicism were reluctant to abandon the field. They abhorred the lack of symbolism and ornament in a modernism that found in function and in the nature of the materials used all that could and should be expressed. The modernists fervently believed that only the lean and functional could reflect the contemporary age.

The debate was joined. The immediate impact on classical architecture was to effect a compromise, often referred to as "streamlined," "stripped," or the more Depression-like "starved" classicism. Buildings in the style were basically formal and symmetrical, but they decreasingly incorporated classical detail. In retrospect, it was a symbolic recipe for economically lean times.[22]

Several important Nashville buildings typify this transitional style of architecture, most of them made for the functions of government. The earliest was the Main Branch of the U.S. Post Office on Broadway (fig. 2.35), designed in 1934 by Marr and Holman. Although basically characterized by the suave, streamlined look of the Art Deco style, the massive block is incised by fluted pilasters, while stylized eagles—a national symbol and also the symbolic bird of Zeus/Jupiter—stand like centurions at the building's main entrances.

Eakin School (fig. 2.36) clearly illustrates the suppression of classical detail in the emerging modern period, perhaps because it carries less obvious associations with the national government. Designed by Tisdale & Pinson in 1935, the building's entrance court features a colonnade, but the facade's pilasters are generic rather than identifiable with any ancient order.

The massive Davidson County Courthouse of 1937 (fig. 2.37) was the fifth

2.32 American National Bank, 1926

First American National Bank

courthouse to occupy pride of place on Nashville's public square. Architects Emmons Woolwine of Nashville and Frederick C. Hirons of New York responded to the need to project the solidity of local authority by designing a solid block of a building embellished by heroically scaled Doric columns and a Roman-inspired cornice, complete with bull heads and serpents. The forecourt features two large fountains that are among the best examples of Art Deco work in the city.

Similar in character but considerably smaller than the courthouse is the Tennessee State Supreme Court Building (fig. 2.38). Built in 1937 to the design of architects Marr & Holman, it is an extremely formal and dignified building that retains a classical proportion and symmetry composed of the basic classical elements. These elements are, however, simplified of ornament, except for the richly detailed cornice. The transitional nature of the Supreme Court's architecture is particularly evident in the interior, where a vivid Art Deco character is subtly blended with a vague classicism.

2.33 War Memorial Building, 1925
Photograph: Charles W. Warterfield, Jr.

The John Sevier State Office Building (fig. 2.39) breaks away from the rectangular temple format in an effort to embrace a difficult corner site and to address directly the then-existing War Memorial Square (since replaced by Legislative Plaza). Mostly Art Deco in detail, the greatly enriched main cornice is Nashville's last expression of a Beaux-Arts classical character.

An attempt to maintain the classical theme of the State of Tennessee government complex of buildings after the caesura of World War II, the Tennessee State Library and Archives (fig. 2.40) was designed by architect H. Clinton Parrent in 1952. In light of Nashville's belated acceptance of modernism for the design of major buildings, Parrent's salute to classicism appears half-hearted. Although the facade features a portico of six Greek Ionic columns, in themselves correctly detailed, the porch's shallowness and the bland block to which it is attached are timid gestures—too little and too late.

*2.34 War Memorial
Building, sculpture court*
Photograph: Charles W.
Warterfield, Jr.

Proponents had valid reasons for the continued incorporation of classical symbols and values into the architecture of government in the 1930s. There was also ancient precedent. In the fifth century B.C., Athens had undertaken a major building program to thank the gods for, and to repair the damage caused by, the city's successful defense against the Persians. Our Depression-era government initiated large construction projects to repair the cultural and economic damage inflicted on our nation by the crash of 1929. Government reiterated the classical style as a way of saying that things would get better, that our foundations were as solid as Western civilization itself.

World War II seemed to place that

civilization directly into American hands. We had designed the economic and military machine that saved Europe for democracy, and we were ready to design the peace that came after. For the American government, that peace was a state of armed truce. The classical past seemed somewhat irrelevant in the face of the Cold War and a possible Armageddon. The American corporations even more firmly abandoned the classical style that had served them well in the past. In this atmosphere the International Style prevailed in the 1950s and 1960s because it spoke a language of motion, not rest. It was not until the late 1970s and 1980s that aspects of post-modern classicism began tentatively to appear.

Classical Quotations

In spite of Nashville's gradual acceptance of modern styles and technologies, its citizens were reluctant to abandon their self-image as a society deeply rooted in tradition. The symbols of the city—the Parthenon and State Capitol, The Hermitage and the other great plantation houses—were and are powerfully evocative reminders of the culture that generated them. Even when Nashville transformed itself into Music City USA, the symbolic architectural high note proved to be an old building—the Ryman Auditorium—not a new one.

Some architects of the period remained well versed in the principles of the classical style because of its popularity for the design of churches and large residences. Order and permanence still had value in the places of private life, the suburbs, and the classical style retreated there with the modern commuter. But classical suburbia embodied little of the symbolism of Nashville's classical past. The porticos and cornices that veneered these essentially modern buildings made a fashion statement, not a value statement.

Among the best of these buildings were a number of churches designed by architects trained in classicism whose practice extended into the modern age. Westminster Presbyterian Church (fig. 2.41), built by Warfield & Keeble Architects in 1937, is a beautifully proportioned, if not unusual, structure, featuring a graceful spire over a Greek Corinthian portico and an interior based on a Roman basilica. The much larger First Presbyterian Church (fig. 2.42) is a 1956 design by Francis B. Warfield. These churches are the best of a genre that descends from the Renaissance through Christopher Wren and thence into the early colonial churches of America.

The Belle Meade branch of the Commerce Union Bank, now Nations Bank (fig. 2.43), is one of the most recent examples of the temple form built in Nashville. A 1950s work by Victor H. Stromquist, its pedimented portico and Federal fanlight transom echo Nashville's earliest banks, and its square, stone columns recall those at the nearby Belle Meade mansion. Significantly, the bank makes its discrete statement of secure wealth in the suburb that, from its beginnings, was designed to embody the stability and permanence of old money wisely spent.

2.35   United States Post Office, main office, 1934
Photograph: Charles W. Warterfield, Jr.

By contrast, the Davidson County Board of Education Administration Building (fig. 2.44) is typical of the attempts in the mid-twentieth century to utilize classical features on

*2.36 Eakin School,
1935*
Photograph: Charles W.
Warterfield, Jr.

*2.37 Davidson County
Courthouse, 1937*
Photograph: Charles W.
Warterfield, Jr.

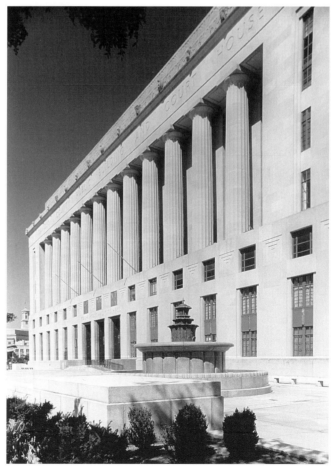

2.38 Tennessee State Supreme Court Building, 1937

2.39 John Sevier State Office Building, 1939

Photographs: Charles W. Warterfield, Jr.

2.40 Tennessee State Library and Archives, 1952

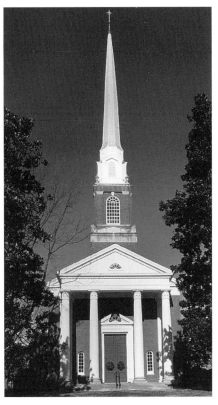

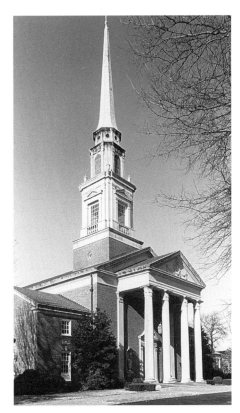

*2.41 (above, l)
Westminster Presbyterian
Church, 1937*

*2.42 (above, r) First
Presbyterian Church,
1956*

*2.43 Nations Bank,
Belle Meade branch
(originally Commerce
Union Bank)*

Photographs: Charles W.
Warterfield, Jr.

73

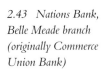

otherwise modern construction. Designed by George Waller in 1953, it represents a widespread trend in educational and institutional buildings of the period. The portico, though fairly well detailed, announces the entrance in a manner in no way integrated into the building's composition. We have come a long way from Strickland's porticos on the State Capitol.

The facade of McKendree Methodist Church (fig. 2.45) is the most recent of a series of expansion and revisions to the original design of 1833 (see fig. 2.7). It was built in 1966 to the design of architects Wilson & Odom.

These buildings incorporate generally accurate reproductions of prototypical classical details. Some Nashville architects of the last half of the twentieth century, however, have chosen to take liberties with them. In the process they have created highly personal and stylized interpretations of classical architecture.

The most well-known for his mannered interpretation of classicism is Edwin Keeble. His Immanuel Baptist Church (fig. 2.46) is composed of conventional elements, modified in idiosyncratic ways. The two-tiered cupola is a highly attenuated form, the urns that mark the corners of the cupola's base are no pattern book reproductions, and the

2.44   Davidson County Board of Education Administration Building, 1953

Photograph: Charles W. Warterfield, Jr.

ocular window in the pediment has a stylized octagonal cast. Height is added to the Greek-style portico by placing its floor below the level of the door, necessitating a curving iron-railed stair to enter. Keeble takes classicism and stretches it vertically and horizontally as if the forms were moldable plastic.

Another unusual departure is the design for the entrance to Pearl-Cohn High School by Hart-Freeland-Roberts (fig. 2.47). Built in 1986 at the height of the post-modern era, the shallow portico consists of Ionic columns arranged in a convex colonnade that recedes into the facade without reference to cornice or pediment. The details of classicism applied to modernism's plastic, space-enclosing forms, rather than the solid space-displacing mass of classicism, makes post-modernism a hyphenated mixture of styles.

The David Lipscomb University Library (fig. 2.48) is a startling example of post-modern classicism. Tuck Hinton Architects designed the building in 1990, subsequent to the firm's master plan for the campus as a whole. In an attempt to extend the classical theme of the campus in modern form, however, the totally innovative columns, pediment, and open courtyard, symmetrically arranged within the building, represent a gesture toward contemporary innovation rather than toward the past.

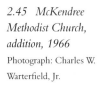

2.45 McKendree Methodist Church, addition, 1966
Photograph: Charles W. Warterfield, Jr.

Designs for chain-store commercial buildings in the post-modern period have increasingly turned to the incorporation of design elements echoing classical shapes, but usually these have communicated only the momentarily marketable or, at best, the most distant of echoes. A case in point is the Holiday Inn, Vanderbilt (fig. 2.49). Its bland modern skin was removed for a 1990 remodelling, and a facade featuring vaguely depressed pediments was applied to the original frame with no more architectural relevance than wallpaper.

A more serious effort to echo Nashville tradition was

2.46 (left) Immanuel Baptist Church

2.47 Pearl-Cohn High School, 1986
Photographs: Charles W. Warterfield, Jr.

2.48 (above) David Lipscomb University Library, 1990

2.49 Holiday Inn, "pediments"

Photographs: Charles W. Warterfield, Jr.

undertaken by the Chicago firm of Kohn, Pedersen & Fox in their Third National Financial Center (now SunTrust Center) of 1985 (fig. 2.50). The towering pedimented roof line, accented by stylized ornaments (acroteria) and jointing, arches over a curving section of glass that suggests a fanlight transom. The sloping (battered) piers of the unroofed entrance portico, enframed within projecting wings, make a direct address to Strickland's Egyptian Revival church across the street.

It is doubtful if Strickland himself would recognize the quotation. We now speak an architectural language in which only an occasional phrase echoes the past, and that but dimly. Classical architecture came to this country because the founders believed that the style could be infinitely and permanently extended in time and place. Strickland crossed the mountains to prove it. What has been proven since is that classicism as an architectural verity is something less than eternal.

Classical Fade-Out

If classicism is slipping from public view in Nashville, it is not merely an issue of new construction. The ironically named "Urban Renewal" projects of the late 1950s, 1960s, and 1970s ensured that much of our collective architectural history, classical or otherwise, would be as "gone with the wind" as the Southern plantation in a previous post-war period. Under the catch-words of "inefficient," "outdated," "uneconomical," and other essentially American expressions of historical intolerance, we have lost the Second Presbyterian Church, the James K. Polk home, and all the Federal and classical townhouses surrounding Capitol Hill. What little remains of Nashville's first suburb, Rutledge Hill, now sits uneasily amidst the metal sheds of small-scale commerce in the shadow of an interstate highway. Our public square is now a parking lot.

The classicism that has defined Nashville's architectural credo for so long now requires that we profess our faith by preserving what we have. The disrespect for history that results in the destruction of our architectural classics has the same lethal logic as book burning. Dynamite and bulldozers permanently take out of circulation stories as necessary to our sense of who we are as *The Iliad* and *The Odyssey, Paradise Lost,* and *Huckleberry Finn.* The architectural fabric of a city's streets is a library of our civic and national culture writ large. Within Nashville's architectural library, the classical tomes have seen the widest and the longest circulation. It is only by preserving them that we retain the ability to read at all.

2.50 Third National Bank Financial Center, now SunTrust, 1985
Photograph: Charles W. Warterfield, Jr.

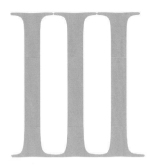

Where We Live

The Classical Style at Home

*If the American artist will study with hope and love the precise thing
to be done by him, considering the climate, the soil, the length of the
day, the wants of the people, the habit and form of the government, he
will create a house in which all these will find themselves fitted, and
taste and sentiment will be satisfied also.*

RALPH WALDO EMERSON

In the early morning fog, the headlights of the cars moving on Harding Road toward downtown Nashville form broad and wavering pools of light on the greasy asphalt. The familiar outlines of suburb and strip mall have become blurred, hidden, and the cars creep along as if explorers in a strange and undiscovered country. For the commuters the fog is a hindrance, but for our journey into history the dissolution of present reality is an unexpected blessing.

We head west, away from town, because we follow in the footsteps of the family for whom the road is named. The Hardings came to Nashville from Virginia, like so many others who decided to take their chances on fame and fortune in the west. Because by 1798 most of the land near to Nashville was already in the hands of men who knew its value, the Hardings looked for less expensive property farther from town. They settled first in the Harpeth River Valley, but in 1807 John Harding purchased "a well-watered 250-acre tract on the east side of Richland Creek, six miles from Nashville. He had seen it countless times as he passed back and forth to town from his father's home on the Harpeth. The road along Richland Creek was an old buffalo trail known as the Natchez Road."[1] It is this same road we take today.

As we reach a section of mortarless limestone wall edging the road on the left, the fringe of trees drops back and a field opens. Even in the fog we can see that it is still a "belle meade" after almost two hundred years. A lane leads gently into it by crossing the flow of Richland Creek and ascending toward the house that is the centerpiece of the beautiful meadow for which it is named. The outlines of the plantation house known as Belle Meade gradually emerge from the mist like a sepia photograph under development (fig. 3.1). The fog has bleached the landscape of color, and what is left are gradations of light and dark. The square pillars topped by plain capitals, the simplified Ionic entablature, the flattened pediment crowned at its apex and corners by the honeysuckle ornament (anthemion acroteria) common to Greece and Rome—all form a limestone skeleton against the solid background of lighter stucco. The fog-induced chiaroscuro

3.1 Belle Meade, facade
Photograph: Charles
W. Warterfield, Jr.

serves to reveal what is most prominent about the classical style of the mid-nineteenth century, a style "bold in silhouette, broad in proportions, and simplified in detail."[2]

To begin at Belle Meade this exploration of the classical style in Nashville's domestic architecture is to open *in medias res*, an appropriate allusion for a classical odyssey. It is also fitting to make a grand entrance with the type of house that comes to mind most immediately when the subject of the classical residence is broached. The Southern plantation house is actually part of a chain of architectural events that leads from Greece and Rome, through Italy and England, to Federal America and the rise of Confederate nationalism, and on to the suburbs and the strip malls. But the columned temples of domesticity still resonate as symbols, occupying the most prominent site in the mental landscape of Southern architectural mythology and creating an expectation for the ideal home that has never been equalled.

It is Belle Meade, and other houses like it, that are the real high water mark of the Old South. Pickett's Charge, the Gettysburg phenomenon that usually carries this tidal metaphor, was the desperate move of a cultural ideal streaming downhill fast.

There is nothing desperate-looking about Belle Meade. In 1853, when extensive remodelling was done to the pre-1840 structure following a fire, when stucco was placed over the brick exterior to make it look like stone, and when the portico of real limestone quarried on the site was added to the facade to make the Belle Meade we know today, the South was in flush times. Cotton was king, and planters made quick wealth out of the raw materials of land and the slaves to work it. Nashville had not yet known the desperate poverty of war, the footprint of Union occupation.

Looking at the facade of Belle Meade today, dreaming in the sunlight that burns off the mist, such events seem unthinkable, even though Nashville thought of little else for decades after the war had ended. In 1853 a home for people of means could still express a confidence unaffected by history, as seemingly oblivious to the passage of time as to the bitter reality of the slave cabins off to the side.

For many, the plantation houses are the quintessential symbol of Old Southern living. And for many, they are a living symbol of slavery, the sad residue of which still stains this land. Both viewpoints are correct, and it is possible to hold them both simultaneously. The existence of the plantation houses depended on an economic system that was essentially inhuman. These houses hold a perennial fascination because they are the clearest articulation of the Old South's characteristic culture, both positive and negative: self-contained, agrarian of ideal and capitalist of practice, class-ridden and slave-dependent, speaking a grandiloquent language derived from a highly selective history.

It is worth exploring what exactly was selected and why. To analyze the grand portico at the end of the drive we must first explore what is meant by classicism in domestic architecture and where it came from on its way to the big house and beyond.

Classicism: From Athens to the Nashville Neighborhood

A significant difference between the classical and what is set up as its contrast, the medieval, has to do with ground plan, with the outline of the masonry on the ground. In classical architecture, according to this analysis, the exterior configuration determines the interior plan, while in the medieval the interior plan determines the exterior configuration.

The plan of the Greek temple, accordingly, maintained its characteristic proportions in order to achieve an ideal exterior balance of length to width, which was roughly two to one in the age of Pericles. The medieval cathedral, to use a contrasting example, had a ground plan determined by all those apses and ambulatories, which create a much more irregular plan that cannot be described in a simple ratio. The reasons for this difference have to do with usage.

The Greek temple was meant to be perceived as sculpture, from the outside, because it was a god house into which only a chosen few priests could go. The medieval cathedral was a god house into which the entire congregation was expected to enter. Inside they found a soaring space in which the light of the everyday was transformed by filters of stained glass. The temple mediated between heaven and earth by its sculptural positioning on or near the most sacred site in the community. The cathedral performed a similar act of mediation by what was within: colored light, flames flickering over the surface of gold and silver screens and vessels, a dark blue ceiling frescoed with stars.

This does not take us very far in the history of Nashville's domestic architecture, but it does describe a general impression we receive when contrasting the outside of a classically inspired residence, such as Belle Meade, with one working with the medievalizing vocabulary that inspired so many nineteenth-century American homes.

The classical home has a blocky symmetry of relatively simple outline, displacing the space it occupies with a forceful confidence, an all-of-a-piece permanence that seeks to transcend time, belying the reality that the Belle Meade we know today actually evolved over decades.

The American Victorian house (fig. 3.2), on the other hand, establishes its legitimacy by the appearance of happening in time. Even though this Eastlake Victorian of 1885 was actually built of-a-piece, its irregularity creates the impression that the current configuration is the result of a process of accretion, that rooms were added, space enclosed, as needed in its history. The more irregular, the older in appearance.

Both types of houses in actuality work from a basic center hall plan. The classical plan balances the two halves, at least of the main block, hiding the asymmetrical wing containing dining area, kitchen, and storeroom out back (fig. 3.3). The Victorian pulls the flanking rooms out of alignment, deliberately refusing the appearance of symmetry. The classical home is resolutely and proudly man-made. The

Victorian is organic in ethos, as if it grew there and might continue to do so.

This contrast has less to do with the strictures of style than with ultimate aims. The classical seeks to dominate its site by setting itself in opposition to it, the Victorian to fit into its site by imitating the complex and highly textured appearance of the natural world.

For those who prefer to "know it when they see it" rather than ponder the abstractions of ground plan, a definition of classicism has to do with motifs, with details of decoration and the proportions of their application. The classical orders, as developed by the Greeks and systematized and recorded by the Romans, announce this approach. The post-and-lintel system of right angles—with an occasional arch thrown in courtesy of the Romans—the column, capital, entablature and pediment, are the building blocks by which classicism is measured.

The resources for these motifs are numerous. Direct observation of actual buildings is the most obvious, but illus-

3.2 Residence of and by Hugh Cathcart Thompson, Holly Street, East Nashville
Photograph: Charles W. Warterfield, Jr.

trations in books played a far more prominent role in the architecture of the United States and by extension, in Nashville. The four books of Palladio (1570), which did so much for Thomas Jefferson, are probably the most famous source for Roman-influenced designs, while the Greeks come into play with *The Antiquities of Athens*. This series of measured delineations, compiled and published by James Stuart and Nicholas Revett (1762-1794), reflect the growing interest in historical accuracy of the classical revival. In the United States, these sources of classicism were transformed

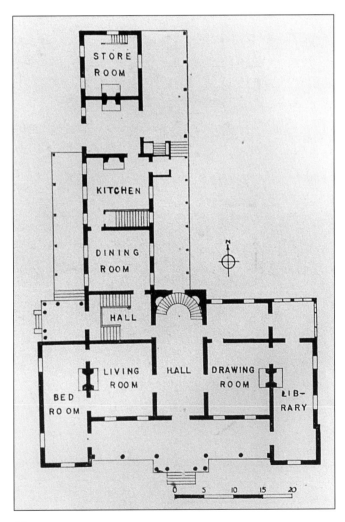

3.3. Belair, plan

Source: Gifford A. Cochran

into practical builders' guides, such as that by Minard Lafever (1833), which demonstrate through measured plans, elevations, and details how to utilize the classical style in meeting current American needs for public and private building (fig. 3.4).

The problems with a reliance on motifs to define what is classical are as numerous as the sources for them. As an imitation of a specific example from Greece or Rome, the definition of what is classical would not apply to much that came after.

The Greeks and Romans themselves applied the classical orders in different ways at different times, allowing us to make distinctions between Archaic, Golden Age, and Hellenistic periods for Greece; Republican, Augustan, and Late Imperial for Rome. The Italians of the Renaissance adapted classical motifs to create something new, and the same is true for Palladio and his followers in England and later America. Essentially, the classical tradition is cumulative rather than consistent, so that it meant to the nineteenth century not only the works of antiquity and the Italian Renaissance, but subsequent work in France and England.

If the tradition were not cumulative it would be a corpse, a thing of the past lacking any value for the needs of the present. As the architectural critic Michael Greenhalgh explains, "One useful property classicism was believed to possess was its rationality, in that its main precepts can be expressed as a series of easily explained rules and models [hence the builders' guides]. If it could be understood by the mind, extrapolated into a system, subjected to rules and measurements, then it could be taught, and passed from generation to generation."[3]

3.4 Classical doorway, elevation and plan

Source: Minard Lafever, *The Modern Builder's Guide.*

Another crucial difficulty with definition by motif is that it tells us so little about style and intention. As Greenhalgh points out with regard to the seventeenth-century architect Gianlorenzo Bernini, "He certainly knew as much about the antique as did any of his great forbears (except Palladio); and much of his architecture is an exuberant working out of antique motifs. But the manner in which he does this produces an architecture that is baroque rather than classical in style and effect. . . ."[4]

This point is especially well taken when discussing the residential architecture of Nashville, which is even more remote from ancient sources and does not bear scrutiny as a mimetic art. To define classical Nashville houses based on principles of correctness would tell little about them.

Under these circumstances, a definition of classicism must abstract the principles that informed the original classics, as all revivalists did, and then apply them to the American home.

What is of interest, then, about the classical homes of Nashville is, again to quote Greenhalgh:

What Classicism is always about—namely the revival and reworking of past ideas and styles, and their fitting to modern circumstances. Ideas are important—much more important than mere motifs, which cannot receive the oxygen of acceptance without the understanding of successive generations of what motifs actually meant—or, at least, what new meanings they can bear. . . . In other words, forms are carriers of meanings. . . . Only rarely has the ideal of Classicism been applied without some attendant ideology; hence Classicism is not merely a range of styles, but rather a way of perceiving the world and using the arts to persuade others to see it in a similar fashion.[5]

While we expect to find a column, a capital, and an entablature when we place the seal of classicism on a building, we expect something less tangible as well. "Classicism *qua* state of mind," says Greenhalgh, "is an approach to the arts that emphasizes the ideal in form and in content over the every-day; the power of reason over the often misleading emotions—and hence restraint, moderation, and self-control; clarity and simplicity—and usually understatement over prolixity; measurability as an index of beauty over intuition; and respect for tradition (hence conservatism and intellectualism)."[6]

As an example, let us return to our comparison of the plantation house (fig. 3.5) and the Eastlake Victorian (fig. 3.2). The home known as Belair (or Belle Air) was built by John Harding of Belle Meade for his daughter Elizabeth, who married Joseph Clay of Kentucky. It was a plain Federal dwelling to which wings, a classical porch, and a gallery were added in 1838 by later owner William Nichol.[7]

Elevations of the front facades of the two houses articulate the differences that we have already considered previously with a comparison of the ground plans. Belair is a series of carefully subordinated hierarchies, main house to wings, classical portico with pediment to unroofed gallery and porch. The columns of the first level porch are in the Doric order, the second level in the Ionic, maintaining the hierarchy of orders established on the Colosseum in Rome. Belair is a building that even the outsider can rationally apprehend.

3.5 Belair, facade
Photograph: Charles W.
Warterfield, Jr.

The Eastlake Victorian, on the other hand, refuses rational symmetry in place of a seemingly natural irregularity. In contrast to Belair's hierarchically arranged series of voids enclosed by a pair of solids, the Eastlake facade steps back from right to left. The central tower is flanked, not by two symmetrical wings, but by a gable projecting to the right, and a gable set at a ninety-degree angle to the left. The spaces pulled forward to prominence on the right are actually not the most important ones, containing the everyday parlor on the first level and a small bedroom on the second, while the public parlor and main bedroom are on the left, concealed behind the asymmetrically placed porch on the first level and a small dormer on the second. The way this house works cannot be read from its facade; it is for insiders to comprehend.

The Eastlake Victorian's ornament also lacks the clarity, restraint, and sense of tradition of Belair's. There is no obvious intellectual precedent for the elaborate eave brackets, hood moldings over windows, sunburst pediment over the door, for the lathe-turned posts and spools on the porch. The solid planarity of the walls of Belair dissolves, in the 1885 house, under a textured onslaught of ornament. If the classicism of Belair represents an ideal of Nature as susceptible to measurement and rules, then the Eastlake Victorian represents a natural world in which each entity has its own organic integrity that is not susceptible to geometry.

The choice of classicism as a house style, then, predicates an agreed upon set of values that privileges simplicity over complexity, order over extravagance, history over the organic, the ideal over the real. The specific vehicle Nashville's classicists chose to express these values has its unlikely roots in the places of ancient pantheism.

The Temple Form
When William Giles Harding enlarged Belle Meade and added a classical portico in 1853, he was not reviving an ancient form of residential architecture. Greek houses, like

Roman ones, were built around a courtyard or atrium and faced inward, without the public gesture of a columned facade. "There was very little architectural embellishment to the exterior of a Greek house," says Vanderbilt University classical scholar Barbara Tsakirgis. "And there were no grounds or yard except for the courtyard."[8]

The adaptation Harding and other Americans were making first appeared in the Italian Renaissance with the suburban villas of the Veneto.

The shape that these Renaissance villas took utilized a classical Roman building type dislocated from its original function. According to architectural historian Michelangelo Muraro, characteristic elements of the Renaissance villa include a triangular pediment, colonnaded loggia, and decoration depicting pagan agrarian deities, elements that would, during the Roman Empire, have been appropriate for a temple to an agricultural deity. But in the Renaissance villa the temple form is "intended to magnify the virtues of one's own family."[9] The villa has become a temple to family wealth and secular glory.

This choice of the temple form for a country house became a language translatable into many tongues with the works of Andrea Palladio (1508-80). For an antiquarian such as he, domestic architecture was initially a problem, for there was no truly reliable knowledge of Roman town-houses or villas until the eighteenth century. Palladio surmounted it by drawing antique remains and developing designs for houses and villas incorporating them. His demonstration of how to apply antique temple fronts onto domestic architecture ensured that he would be the most influential of all architects.[10]

Palladio's choice of the temple form might have been based in part on what remained to be copied; nevertheless, it is superficially an odd choice. Greek and Roman temples were god houses for a pantheon that had been rejected by Christianity as primitive superstition. And the very success of the temple as a place of repository for the cult image and corresponding treasury of offerings mitigated its usage in daily life: bad acoustics, only two barn-like rooms with little light or ventilation, a peristyle of columns that would break any budget.

What the temples of the ancient world did have was that quality most beloved of real estate agents: location, location, location. Situated on the most sacred sites in town, these god houses were what the community figuratively—and, in the case of the acropolis of Athens, literally—looked up to.

The temple's sacred positioning originally reflected its role as the staple between heaven and earth. But the gods of the ancient heaven no longer had more than literary value for Christianity. The temple was a vessel from which had leached the content of original meaning, into which another meaning could be poured. The aspiring class of the Veneto, newly rich with the profits of banking and trade, stood ready to pour the libations of their wealth, and their personal and dynastic pretensions, into the empty form. They were ready to be figuratively looked up to as well.

As the centers of trade and wealth moved northward and westward, the house-as-temple went with them, to France and then Great Britain. In England, the primary source of domestic architectural styles for the colonies that became the United States, Inigo Jones in the seventeenth century created, almost single-handedly, a classical style in such works as the Queen's House in Greenwich. This inspired the Palladian Revival of Lord Burlington in the early eighteenth century, and both laid the groundwork for the explosion of classical country houses that ensued. The work of Jones and Lord Burlington had the effect of liberating classicism from the Italian peninsula and from the European Continent as a whole, launching it as a "language of expression easily adaptable to local circumstances."[11]

Washington and Jefferson: Architects of the American Temple

The local circumstances of England's American colony were similar to those in the Mother Country, in that people making money wanted to express their enhanced circumstances through the houses in which they lived. But, as the architectural historian Don Gifford points out, there were limits to Colonial American circumstances that set them apart. "Central among the necessities that conditioned Colonial architecture was economy; there was a great deal of building to be done in a short time and with a short supply of labor. Farms, villages and towns could not be inherited; they had to be built; and those who built them then had to turn to other pursuits."[12]

One American who was regularly asked to turn to other pursuits was George Washington. While his circumstances cannot be considered typical, Washington's very prominence ensured that he, and the house he built for himself, would serve as prototypes for the possible in the New World.

"It is often forgotten that Washington, embalmed in history as the Father of our Country, was also an English country gentleman," notes architectural historian Mills Lane. "Like so many Virginia planters, he was obliged to be concerned with practical, everyday cares, including the design and construction of buildings."[13] Washington, like Thomas Jefferson after him, spent some forty years enlarging his house on the Potomac. The property had been in his family since the seventeenth century. His father built a story-and-a-half frame cottage on the plantation in the 1730s, which Washington had stripped to its wooden frame and to which he added a story. He covered the exterior with rusticated boards that simulated masonry in their bevelled edges and in the mixing of sand with the paint that covered them. His reworking of the original structure is characteristic of the evolution of many American plantation houses, and it is a pattern we see in Tennessee. It indicates, nevertheless, a respect for ancestry worthy of a Roman republican.

Enlargements to Mount Vernon continued even during the Revolution. Because these additions were not family rooms, they appear to belie Washington's earlier claim that simple country living was his cherished dream. The new

94

library and banquet hall were prophetically grand enough for his use as first president of the United States. The expansion of Mount Vernon is made still more curious by the fact that George and Martha were childless. It is as if for Washington his house expressed not a personal dynastic ambition but a national one. "Transcending the usual functions of a southern plantation," architectural historian Kenneth Severens says, "Mount Vernon became a symbol of the transformation of Colonial America into an independent republic."[14]

The colossal portico erected on the east facade in 1777 exemplifies this transformation. Its square columns were not architecturally sophisticated, nor were they patterned after English sources. From every point of view the portico is additive, yet it serves to integrate the successive building campaigns into a formal design that aspires beyond the house's humble origins. The portico's two-story height, according to Severens "the first of its kind in American domestic architecture,"[15] became the distinguishing feature of the antebellum plantation house.

With Thomas Jefferson, architecture became aggressively linked to the development of the republic. Jefferson viewed architecture as a matter of public policy and set out, through his own designs, "to improve the taste of my countrymen, to increase their reputation, to reconcile to them the respect of the world and procure them its praise."[16]

The most distinctively personal plantation house of the Colonial and Federal periods, Monticello reflects an architectural theory that is inseparable from Jefferson's political philosophy: the underlying concept of the necessity for rational change, which is also central to the Declaration of Independence. Begun in 1769, Monticello underwent a series of "rational changes" during the course of its construction, deconstruction, and reconstruction. For the rationality crucial to an architecture in evolution, Jefferson went back to the *Quattro libri dell' archittetura* of Palladio, to the Palladian villas he visited on a trip to England in 1786, and to the neoclassicism he observed as minister to France from

1785 to 1789. He adapted these models to his mountain top, drawing on the earthy colors and textures of brick and designing polygonal and rectangular projections to soften his villa's profile, allowing the masonry to complement the landscape.

In spite of his idiosyncratic approach, Jefferson intended for Monticello to be "exemplary of how Americans should live: formal in its Old World sources, yet romantic in its relation to nature; and high style in its cultivation of the arts, yet scientific in its technological gadgetry. . . . Monticello was to the Piedmont what a cultivated plantation was to the wilderness—a willful testament of man's presence amid primeval nature."[17]

While Mount Vernon is less overtly classical than is Monticello, both of these founding homes reflect an ideology for which the classical ethos was appropriate, and which, as a result, became ideals of American life. Mount Vernon's grand but simple rectangular block, with its homey gables and belvedere, speaks the language of a gentleman-amateur who finds virtue in what Washington himself named as his domestic goal: "the republican style of living."[18] One of the colony's weapons against the British Parliament had been a refusal to consume—abstaining from tea and other luxuries marked a colonist as a patriot—and Mount Vernon's dignified but not ornate exterior reflects this rebellion against the conspicuous consumption of monarchy.

Monticello is infinitely more sophisticated in its plan and elevation and their reliance on high style precedents, yet it also reflects architectural choices made in the light of a larger philosophy. To a mainly Protestant country that nevertheless wanted to keep the politics of religion out of the politics of government, the classical style, long divorced of religious content, was a style much more appropriate than anything medieval, with its Catholic overtones. To a patriotism that used as verbal metaphors the heroes of the Greek democracies and the republic of Rome to meet current nationalistic needs, the architectural style of those ancient patriots was a fitting visual metaphor for the new country. These choices of metaphors the founders made more or less consciously.

There are, however, less obvious reasons for the choice of the classical, and they have to do with the classical style's implicit ideology. We have already discussed the way that the classical reliance on symmetry and hierarchy expresses a belief in an order that can only be extracted from the apparent chaos of nature by human will. This belief in the virtues of the man-made may seem naive to us today, as we watch woodlands gobbled up by subdivisions and strip malls. An orderly domestic life, however, was especially important to a people who worked diligently to replace randomness and wildness with walls and fences.

This belief in architecture as an expression of order takes on particular urgency when we remember, as we are urged to do by the historian Roger Kennedy, that in one area of their lives eighteenth-century Americans "had assaulted order and invited chaos: their politics were at variance with their domestic behavior. They had committed symbolic patricide. The king is the father of his people and they had rebelled against their king. . . . They had committed the ultimate act of public disorder, and they knew from their Shakespeare" that that sort of crime does not pay well the body politic.[19] The classical style of the Colonial and Federal periods can be seen as a hedge against that disorder, a way to impose self-control and authority on a country as it expanded westward.

The Temple in Tennessee

If first President George Washington expected to find at Mount Vernon "more happiness in retirement than I ever experienced amidst a wide and bustling world,"[20] the same is true of the first president from the west, Andrew Jackson. Jackson's sentiments, written during a Senatorial sojourn in the District of Columbia in the 1820s, are remarkably similar to those of the Founding Father. "How often [do] my thoughts lead me back to the Hermitage. There in private life, surrounded by a few friends, would be a paradise compared to the best situation here; and if once more there it would take a writ of *habeas corpus* to remove me into public life again."[21]

What it actually took, of course, was Jackson's election to the presidency in 1828. The Hermitage is Tennessee's Mount Vernon. The symbolic weight both houses carry far exceeds their respective architectural merits. Both also embody the same inherent contradiction between the ideal and the real: the simple life of republican virtue was supported by the much greater austerity of life among slaves. Both citizens were called from their fields to defend their country, though neither was a Cincinnatus; someone else was pushing the plow.

The Hermitage was not the first classical house in Nashville. What makes it architecturally more significant than others has less to do with its presidential pedigree than with the fact that it is a microcosm, in its various stages of development, of the history of domestic architecture on the frontier.

Unlike Washington and Jefferson, Jackson did not build his home on ancestral acres. His father died before he was born, and when Jackson emigrated from the Carolinas to Nashville in 1788 he was a young man with more ambition than wealth. Before he purchased the land on which he was to build the Hermitage, Jackson had already farmed two other tracts of land, the second of which he was forced to sell to pay off debts.

In spite of Jackson's profession of love for the private life of The Hermitage, his wealth was rooted in the public arena. He first made money as a lawyer when trained students of the law were few and far between in the territory. Legal contacts led to his engagement in land speculation, and he also did business in a general store, a racecourse, a tavern, and a boatyard. His political reputation was based on his career as a professional soldier, fighting to rid the new country of the British as well as the Native Americans. Jackson, then, was not an agrarian until he could afford to be one.

98

The first dwelling on the Hermitage plantation was a log house, which Jackson, like the Hardings of Belle Meade, occupied until he had the funds for a more substantial structure. In 1819 Jackson employed Henry Reiff to build a brick dwelling. From what we know of it from bad reproductions (fig. 3.6), it was a plain Federal rectangle of a house with four rooms on each floor divided by a central hall.

The Federal style, named to distinguish it from its English forbears after independence, was the first high-style architectural language used in Nashville. Characterized by a delicacy and slenderness of detail unknown to the Romans, it derived from the classical revival work of the Adam brothers in England. In Tennessee it consisted mostly of a system of small-scale copies of classical details. The only stylish detail on Jackson's house, however, was a fanlight over the front door, although some illustrations also include a simple, one-story porch. This 1819 Hermitage was a house that still bore the marks of a defensive frontier posture, a simple block with embellishments restricted to the interior.

In 1831, with the marriage of his adopted son, Jackson

3.6 The Hermitage of 1819

Source: Stanley Horn, *The Hermitage of Old Hickory.*

prepared the Hermitage mansion for the couple by adding projecting one-story wings placed symmetrically on each end, and a connecting one-story colonnade across the front between the projecting wings, with a temple-form second story portico at its center to give focus to the entrance and provide an upstairs porch (fig. 3.7). This Hermitage probably inspired the extant building of Belair (see above, fig. 3.5), which today conveys most accurately its appearance.

In drawing parallels between Washington and Jackson, it is noteworthy that the two wings of Jackson's addition had the same functions as the primary additions Washington made to Mount Vernon: a library and a dining room. It is also worth noting that Washington ordered for his banquet room a mantelpiece that depicted the departure of Aeneas from Troy, while Jackson added to the new Hermitage a wallpaper that depicted the tale of Telemachus, son of Odysseus. These presidents were nothing if not self-conscious about their familiarity with the classics.

For the additions, Jackson hired an architect, David Morrison, whom the architectural historian James Patrick calls

3.7 The Hermitage of 1831

Source: Stanley Horn, *The Hermitage of Old Hickory.*

"Tennessee's first architect of the Greek Revival."[22] While the symmetrical wings, Doric columns, temple-form porch, and hierarchical massing establish the Hermitage as a Greek Revival building, the fanlight over the entrance is a Federal holdover. Taken as a whole the 1831 Hermitage lacks the monumentality that characterizes the bolder Greek Revivalism of nearby Tulip Grove, built for Rachel Jackson's nephew and completed in 1836 (fig. 3.8).

Tulip Grove is not ambiguous in its classical aspirations. The monumental two-story temple-form portico is bold in its archaeologically correct usage of the Doric column and frieze, leading Patrick to call it "the principal domestic monument of the local Greek Revival."[23]

The employment of the colossal order at Tulip Grove foreshadows the last Hermitage, the one we know today (fig. 3.9). Constructed after an 1834 fire had gutted all but one of the wings, the fourth Hermitage is what Patrick describes as "the first monument of southern nationalism in Tennessee."[24] This is a good description, in that it distinguishes the architectural celebration of the flush times of the 1840s and 1850s, the theme of which was columns, from earlier versions of the classical spirit. "Federal and Grecian houses," Patrick tells us, "gave way to a self-conscious architecture

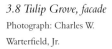
3.8 Tulip Grove, facade
Photograph: Charles W. Warterfield, Jr.

that combined classical principles of symmetry and proportion with a disregard for antique precedent and a baroque assertiveness."[25]

While the mixed agricultural economy of Tennessee did not yield the bonanza of sudden wealth as freely as did the cotton fields of Mississippi and Louisiana, the decades immediately preceding the Civil War were, nevertheless, prosperous times indeed. This prosperity was expressed in an architecture whose amplified columns recalled the temples of Greece and Rome as self-consciously as Southern politicians recalled the slavery that existed in the *polis* of Greece and the republic of Rome. Although in fact planters were capitalists whose funds were invested in land and slaves, its builders strove to idealize an aristocratic agrarian order.

It is fitting that Andrew Jackson, a frontier adventurer for whom agrarianism was just one among many adventures, anticipated the architecture of Southern nationalism in his rebuilding of the Hermitage. His entire career was in many ways a defiant gesture to the North and the East, proclaiming the new country to the southwest as a power to be reckoned with.

3.9 The 1834 Hermitage today
Photograph courtesy of
The Hermitage

The contract between Jackson and the builders, Joseph Reiff and William Hume, indicates that the original intention was to rebuild the Morrison Hermitage unchanged, which is probably why there was no architect for this version. When it was all finished, however, the portico alone, with its six tall fluted columns crowned with cast-iron acanthus leaves, had cost more than 10 percent of the expenditure for the entire rebuilding. The columns of the front facade recall ancient temples, but the pediment is concealed behind the entablature, a departure from antique precedent that would reappear often during these antebellum decades. The effect is to emphasize the columns by downplaying their obvious connection to the less grand building behind. This device is peculiarly notable at the Hermitage, where the front portico, when viewed from the side (fig. 3.10), seems tenuously attached, possessing a false-front quality we tend to associate with movie sets.

3.10 The Hermitage of 1834, side elevation
Photograph: Charles W. Warterfield, Jr.

Why did Jackson not rebuild the Hermitage of David Morrison as he had originally planned? There are no clear-cut surviving testaments. The fourth Hermitage was constructed during the period when Jackson served as President, and perhaps he, like Washington before him, built a colossal portico not merely for himself, but for the nation. In support of this theory we can note that Jackson left The Hermitage to his adopted son, with the proviso that should it ever be put up for sale, it be offered first to the state of Tennessee.[26] This provision suggests that Jackson saw his home as having a public character that transcended its private function.

In any case, the front columns of the Hermitage are one of the more extreme examples of putting on "a face to meet the faces that we meet." Palladio more or less invented this gesture for the residence, but it was an especially fitting one for a self-consciously emerging region. As a general appropriation of a classicism that had had much to do with legitimizing independence, the portico anticipates parallels between that separation and the separateness that Southerners were beginning to feel as their culture and economic system came under increasing scrutiny. As the invention of a new architectural tradition whose subject was the column, it served rhetorically to enhance Southern distinctiveness.

The architecture of Southern nationalism is an emotion-laden one in part because of the pathos or tragedy, depending on one's viewpoint, of a style and a culture that did not fade away but went down with all flags flying. If the plantation architecture of white pillars had had a natural run like other styles, it probably would not have retained the same resonance. But the columnar style also has an emotional content because it deliberately spoke, at the time of its development, an emotional language, an "I'm in charge here" departure from the self-control of previous classicism. Even today we cannot approach the white columns of a plantation house without being startled by the contrast between them and the natural world beyond. To imagine them at their time of construction, when the surroundings were even more "natural," is to grasp even more fully their quality of self-dramatization.

Breaking the Classical Boundaries: Belmont

Self-dramatization came as naturally as breathing to the patron of Belmont. Had Adelicia Acklen not existed, someone would have invented her, so colorful is the narrative of her life. Scarlett O'Hara has nothing on the woman who built Belmont, whose life, among other notable features, included three husbands and a presentation at the Second Empire court of Napoleon III and Eugenie. During the Civil War, some shrewd double-dealings with Yankees and Confederates alike salvaged a Louisiana cotton crop that realized $960,000 in gold (approximately $2 million in greenbacks) on the Liverpool market. This maneuver allowed Acklen to maintain her lavish lifestyle at a time when the war had brought most planters to their economic knees.

It was the pre-war boom in cotton that made possible the construction of Belmont (originally Belle Monte) in the early 1850s. The terms of an 1849 marriage contract with her second husband, Joseph Acklen, guaranteed that Adelicia's properties would be under her control. By breaking the will of her first husband, Isaac Franklin, in 1852, Adelicia ensured that she had properties to control, specifically, 8,700 acres of cotton land in Louisiana. A mansion to flaunt such wealth was a natural evolution.

True to Roman and later Italian Renaissance precedents for the villa form, Joseph and Adelicia Acklen first built Belmont as a suburban summer home, wintering in their Nashville townhouse when not on their Louisiana estates. After an 1859 remodelling, however, Belmont became the family's principal residence.

An 1880 article in the *Nashville Daily American* describes the villa as "built after the plan of the Borghese Palace at Rome,"[27] a summer house constructed on the hill called the Pincio in 1632. This was during the flowering of the Roman Baroque, the style that reworked classical motifs into a newly aggressive posture at the behest of the Counter-Reformation. The 1859 reworking of Belmont was designed by Adolphus Heiman, an architect whose public commissions included designs in the classical and Gothic styles, but whose own home showed a preference for the Italianate.

The Belmont of 1859 (fig. 3.11) is composed of a central two-story block crowned with a belvedere, in which a porch supported by two composite (combining Ionic and Corinthian motifs) columns is recessed between flanking walls defined by pilasters. The planes of these flanking walls of the main block are broken by projecting one-story porches topped by balustrades. Symmetrical one-story wings are set behind the facade and textured, like the balcony of the central porch, with cast iron ornament. The ground plan, while resolutely symmetrical, is marked by a complexity uncharacteristic of the strictly classical (fig. 3.12). In elevation the massing is also complex, marked by a dynamic rhythm of recession, projection, and recession that builds towards the culminating belvedere.

Deference is shown to the classical love of symmetry, hierarchy, and precedent, but the composition of Belmont as a whole shows little direct inspiration from the Greek Revival. The interior cornices and brackets, colored glass, and round-headed windows in the ballroom define even more clearly the turning of the architectural vocabulary away from classicism, and towards the Italianate, a romantic language with medieval rather than classical roots.

The grounds of Belmont serve as a foil for the white columns and pilasters of the villa by exploring picturesque possibilities.[28] A painting of the estate (fig. 3.13) presents the suburban plantation—Belmont was never intended to be a self-supporting farm—as a romantically landscaped park featuring, in addition to the villa, an art gallery, summer houses,

3.11 Belmont, facade

Photograph: Charles W. Warterfield, Jr.

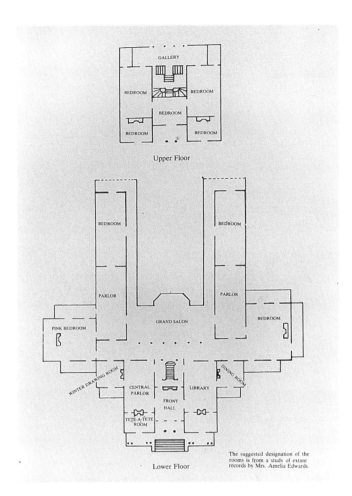

3.12 Belmont, plan
Source: Albert W. Wardin,
Jr., *Belmont Mansion: the
Home of Joseph and Adelicia
Acklen*

GALLERY

BEDROOM   BEDROOM

BEDROOM

BEDROOM   BEDROOM

Upper Floor

BEDROOM   BEDROOM

PARLOR   PARLOR

GRAND SALON   BEDROOM

PINK BEDROOM

WINTER DRAWING ROOM   DINING ROOM

CENTRAL   LIBRARY
PARLOR

FRONT
HALL

TETE-A-TETE
ROOM

Lower Floor

The suggested designation of the
rooms is from a study of extant
records by Mrs. Amelia Edwards.

*3.13 Belmont, painting by
an anonymous artist*
Source: Cheekwood Museum
of Art

107

water tower, greenhouses, menageries, a lake, and statuary. The formality and symmetry of the house gradually give way to an informality and irregularity in the grounds, in a manner that Andrew Jackson Downing, America's prophet of the picturesque, would have admired.

With Belmont the architecture of Southern nationalism had reached its final phase. The house and grounds articulate the departure from the stability and self-control of classicism towards an aggressive display of wealth intended to promote the taste and cultivation of its patrons. Despite the pronounced centrality of the composition, simplicity and order exist in tension with complexity and extravagance.

Belmont breaks the smooth planes of classicism just as the South was pushing the outer limits of the ideology that classicism expressed. While there are clear differences among the three masonry Hermitages, and between the Hermitage and other antebellum classical houses in Nashville, all express an agreed upon set of values that Belmont begins to forego.

The choice of tradition over innovation was important at a time when the United States was insecure about its own cultural validity. For a Southern culture full of swagger, however, an innovative use of tradition was a more important rhetorical stance. The choice of reason over emotion was appropriate to a time when the country felt the need to assert the rationality of its very existence, but less appropriate for a region making its case at fever pitch. The choice of a man-made simplicity and clarity was a necessary antidote to the surrounding wilderness, but unnecessary for a Belmont genteelly sited in the suburbs. The idealization of an agrarian aristocracy through the houses it lived in was a desirable enhancement of the Jacksonian realities of agrarian capitalism. The Belmont estate was never a source of wealth, however, but an expression of wealth dislocated from its source in the fields of Louisiana. Belmont is a picturesquely enhanced classicism set amidst a picturesquely controlled nature. America, philosophically speaking, was moving from town and country into the suburbs.

The newest Hermitage had been standing less than two years when Amos Kendall, a visitor to the estate who was a member of Jackson's cabinet, wrote in 1837, "Everything at the Hermitage looks perennial, permanent."[29] That is exactly how it was supposed to look; Kendall got the classical message.

In contrast, the impressions of Mother Frances Walsh of the Dominican Sisters, a visitor to Belmont between 1860 and 1863, were of the latest fashions in self-conscious splendor. She records interior "surroundings suggestive of Oriental luxury" and a landscape of "sylvan loveliness . . . arranged as by the hand of a master artist."[30] The message of Belmont came from a South that perceived itself as aggressively in motion toward nationhood. Traditions die when their utility is no longer recognized. For the South on the eve of war, the classical spirit had outlived its usefulness.

The Classical Option: Nashville Suburbia

As post-Civil War Nashville began to fill up with the physical and moral detritus of the Industrial Revolution, others dependent on the commerce of capitalism followed Adelicia Acklen's model and made for themselves a private space set in distinction to the public places where their wealth was made. They chose for this purpose the areas surrounding the commercial center, once farmland now accessible by public and private transport to men of business, men who could afford to shake the city dust from their feet of an evening and seek respite at the family hearth presided over by the womanly "angel of the house." The commuter was born.

The styles of these early suburban dwellings carry further the departure from the strictly classical that we have already seen in Belmont. If the point was to distinguish between public and private life, then these new houses would be unlikely to continue in a classical vein noted for its identification with the public life of the ancients. The Gothic, Italianate, Eastlake, and Queen Anne styles reflected a need, not for the man-made in distinction to wilderness, but for the organic in distinction to the man-made wilderness of the modern city. The style of the Greeks and the Romans did not meet the needs of private life.

It would take a new self-consciousness about national and local history before classical would again be desirable as a home-style. The celebration of the U.S. Centennial in 1876 inspired a revival that recalled, for the first time, not the history of other nations but of our own. This American revival saw the simple symmetries of the classical block reappear, embellished by the fanlights and multi-pane windows of the Colonial and Federal periods of a hundred years before, when the nation as a nation began. After the "something new" architectural ornament that the prosperous had most conspicuously consumed during the Victorian period, the elite now sought a return to a more discrete and orderly style, self-confident enough to embrace the gentility of something old. Yet the classical style did not dominate the architectural market as it had in the early decades of our nation. Now the American Colonial and Federal versions of classicism were simply part of the options in residential architecture, historic styles among many that we citizens could claim for a country beginning to think of itself as the latest in a distinguished line of owners of Western civilization.

A good example of classicism chosen for an early residential suburb is actually not a house at all. The Holly Street Fire Hall of 1914 is a public building designed to fit itself into its East Nashville neighborhood with a style that would not have been inappropriate for an imposing single-family home (fig. 3.14). Nashville continued this tradition of home-like fire halls with the later Tudor bungalow fire station on Hillsboro Road and the ranch fire hall on Davidson Road in West Meade.

The Holly Street Fire Hall is an example of turn-of-the-century classicism, when grand columns and pediments

3.14 Holly Street Fire Hall

Photograph: Charles W. Warterfield, Jr.

added an expansive weight to the Colonial and Federal language of residence by means of the Écoles des Beaux-Arts. The teachings of this Parisian school formed the basis for the American City Beautiful Movement, which used the classical style to give dignity and rationality to cities suffering from an excess of *laissez faire*. The Columbian Exposition of 1893 in Chicago gave to the nation not only examples of the Beaux-Arts style but also the reason for its use. According to architectural historian Don Gifford,

> *The fair's motto was 'Not Matter, But Mind,' and the fair was advertised (and popularly accepted) as art, for once with money no object. Americans had become accustomed to being regarded and criticized as a people more interested in money than aesthetic values; and the fair was to answer that criticism, to be a demonstration of American aesthetic hunger and an advertisement of achieved aesthetic maturity. . . . The motive of the fair was to sacrifice money in the interests of achieving the higher values of art (it was expected that the fair would lose money).*[31]

Chicago's White City and such offshoots as Tennessee's own Centennial Exposition of 1897 supplied the rationale underlying the American Beaux-Arts classical revival: the assumption that art lies in a realm apart from the realities of

111

an urban, industrial economy. These expositions were impermanent primers in the style, lessons in wood and plaster that were adapted by residential neighborhoods to create in the "not-city" grand avenues flanked by imposing mansions, private temples in which the cult of art, not commerce, was worshipped.

West End Avenue became one of the grandest of boulevards into the suburbs after electric streetcars allowed commuters to leap the railroad gulch to the west of downtown Nashville. A West End residence built around 1915 (fig. 3.15) has a two-story classical portico similar to that of the Holly Street Fire Hall, utilizing monumental Corinthian columns and pediment to establish an imposingly vertical

3.15 Residence, West End Avenue
Photograph: Charles W. Warterfield, Jr.

presence along the promenade. In contrast to the reasonably correct application of classical details to this facade stands a residence immediately next door, which combines a one-story porch supported by vaguely Ionic columns with the broad eaves and gently sloping roof of the four-square and bungalow styles (fig. 3.16). Taken in conjunction, these two houses illustrate the difference between real classical aspiration and the humbler attempt to add a classical detail or two into an essentially homier mixture.

In distinction to West End Avenue, which now has as many fast food stops and strip malls as mansions, there stands one Nashville avenue that has maintained its grandness as a residential promenade. Belle Meade Boulevard, the main thoroughfare of the twentieth-century suburb carved

3.16 Residence, West End Avenue
Photograph: Charles W. Warterfield, Jr.

from the plantation of the Hardings, is "The Boulevard" of choice for old-money Nashville and those who would like their coinage to be perceived as having an antique patina. Along this imposing street, divided by a lavishly landscaped median and edged by large homes with estate-sized grounds, the classical style has long communicated the socially correct message of stability, tradition, and dynasty.

The Belle Meade Boulevard residence designed by the local firm of Asmus & Clark and built in 1926 (fig. 3.17) is one of the better examples of the twentieth-century classical revival carried out by patrons with wealth enough to hire an architect who knew how to use it. For both the West End Avenue and Belle Meade Boulevard houses, the classical style is revived as one traditional house type among many capable of expressing the social values of wealth discretely used, dynasty securely established. Consequently, they lack the more immediate identification with Greek and Roman civilization characteristic of the earlier days of the nation.

3.17 Residence, Belle Meade Boulevard

Photograph: Charles W. Warterfield, Jr.

Classicism for the Dead

The Police Record of the Army of the Cumberland, the Union force that occupied Nashville from 1862 until the war's end, describes the ornamented grounds of Belmont as looking like "a fashionable first-class cemetery."[32] The sneering tone of this commentary reflects a degree of partisan prejudice that reveals a deeper truth. The cemeteries of Nashville, like the Belmont we have described above, are expressions of the picturesque impulse to create a gap between manifestations of wealth and its sources, an impulse that created the American suburbs.

City Cemetery. When we pass through the stone gateposts of Nashville's City Cemetery on Fourth Avenue South, we walk into a suburb of the dead. Since the time of the Romans, at least, burying grounds have been placed outside the city walls, close enough to carry a body from town, but far enough away to avoid contamination of the water supply. The City Cemetery, established in 1822, is the resting place of Nashville firsts—"First Lady Schoolteacher," "First White Male Child"—along with the remains of twenty thousand of Nashville's pioneers and politicians, educators and warriors.

The signs marking its lanes speak the leafy language of streets in the century's small towns and suburbs: Oak and Magnolia, Mulberry and Willow. The nineteenth-century view held that the neighborhoods of the dead should communicate the same message as the neighborhoods of the living. This is the place of green grass and big trees, the place where business as usual, Broadway and Main Street, is out of place. This is the not-city.

Much of nineteenth-century society also thought that the graves of the dead, as much as the pre-war columns and post-war gingerbread of its houses, should flaunt family finances. Not for the well-upholstered Victorians are the flat plaques of today that rest discreetly on the face of the earth. In City Cemetery, iron fences carve out family plots in the same way that they were used to carve out front yards, permanently distinguishing between dynasties. Classical arches and limestone urns designed by the likes of William Strickland demonstrate that here lie Remains of Importance.

Several Nashville antebellum classical residences rather cavalierly claim a Strickland pedigree. Manifestations of the "William Strickland built here" phenomenon, such claims indicate an understandable if retrospective desire on the part of the keepers of a culture to affirm that the culture is worth keeping because it was formed by the hands of the famous, whether those hands were actually laid on the project or not. The City Cemetery tombs of Sarah Ann Gray Walker and John Kane, however, were actually designed by the architect of the Tennessee Capitol. They serve as good examples of a full-blown classicism applied to the permanent resting place.

Like the classical homes of Nashville, which represent not a revival of ancient residential forms but the application of the temple facade to new and private purposes, the classical tombs of City Cemetery are not made in direct imitation of ancient funerary monuments. Rather than the pictures in stone of ancient Greece, with their reliefs of the dearly beloved in the contemplative mood of departure, we find a selection of forms and motifs abstracted from ancient public architecture, worked out in miniature scale for the purposes of semi-private mourning.

The Walker tomb (fig. 3.18), signed by Strickland, carries a date of 1845. Its basic form is that of a Roman arch, like those that marked the ancient triumphs of heroes. The arch's monumental severity is relieved by egg-and-dart molding, scrolls with acanthus volutes, and a dentil cornice. A laurel wreath and a torch with flame permanently frozen in masonry solidify the theme of heroic action, in spite of the reality that Sarah Ann was no warrior or athlete but a bourgeois lady of means.

Strickland's 1850 tomb for John Kane (fig. 3.19) also utilizes monumental forms, here for the sake of a uniquely personal meaning. "Erected by the Stonecutters of the State House," the tomb memorializes one of their own, the head

3.18 Tomb of Sarah Ann Gray Walker, City Cemetery
Photograph: Charles W. Warterfield, Jr.

116

3.19 Tomb of John Kane, City Cemetery
Photograph: Charles W. Waterfield, Jr.

of the crew of stone masons who had worked so diligently to carve the Capitol. Appropriately enough, the Kane tomb is expressive primarily of rock itself. It is in form a massive monolith topped with an egg-and-dart cornice and originally crowned with limestone carvings of the tools of the stone mason. The battered (sloping) sides remind us of Strickland's taste for the Egyptian, a taste revealed more clearly in his design for Downtown Presbyterian Church. The departure from the Greek and Roman for an influence even more ancient was a fitting quotation from a culture that specialized in the cult of the dead.

These two classical tombs, and the many others in City Cemetery lacking the Strickland polish, reveal an ideology that found in the classical style an appropriate vessel for current meanings. The style said that these were not just any dead but the remains of those whose efforts to make a city and a state were the modern equivalents of the patriotism of those who died at Thermopylae, who won honors for their states at the Olympian games, who marched in victory through the Forum. These funerary monuments claim for the builders of our civilization the same heroic status.

The Classical Temple in Its Final Form: Mount Olivet Cemetery. The purest classicism of twentieth-century Nashville is to be found in the houses of the dead. After its founding in 1855, Mount Olivet Cemetery replaced the crowded City Cemetery as the place of final prominence. Belmont's Adelicia Acklen was laid to rest there in a Gothic cottage, which was then the height of funerary fashion. The various surrounding tomb-styles mirror the chronology of architectural taste found in the concurrent residential suburbs.

The mournful motifs of the broken column and the classical urn never lapsed entirely, but it was with the family vaults of the twentieth century that the temple form made its purest and perhaps final comeback. A series of 1920s mausolea in the Doric, Ionic, and Tuscan styles (fig. 3.20, for one example) betray such striking similarities that their origin in

117

a mortuary pattern book seems obvious. These temples to family dot the grounds of Mount Olivet like the treasuries of the city-states on the sacred way at Delphi. The cemetery was perhaps the one place in twentieth-century Nashville where true permanence seemed an achievable goal.

Classical Fragments

Under the more temporal conditions of twentieth century living, as opposed to twentieth-century dying, the classical is found in bits and pieces, like the pentimenti in a decomposing oil painting.

The prominent Nashville architect Edwin Keeble designed machines-for-living for clients devoted to the International Style, but his own taste was "devoted to the classical," according to his widow, Alice. "Keeble classical," however, is an ancient language made new by idiosyncracies that the Mannerists of the late Renaissance would have admired.

For his own home of 1936, Keeble designed a classical pavilion set on the top of a hill in the tradition of Monticello. Keeble built his one-story version of white-painted brick with Corinthian columns and blue trim. Inside (fig. 3.21), Keeble betrays his Beaux-Arts training with a dramatic sight line that travels on an axis from a small, low-ceilinged entry hall through a soaring barrel-vaulted living room to an over-scale window whose shape echoes the arch of the vault. The Doric frieze at the base of the barrel vault has the correct details of triglyphs and metopes, but its lack of integration into the vault or the wall below is rational means used for irrational ends. This room also contains a staircase baluster in which "loops" of metal are made to imitate the gravity fall of cloth (fig. 3.22), another playful gesture of matter working against itself that is characteristic of mannered reworkings of traditions in decline.

3.20 Cheek family tomb, Mount Olivet Cemetery
Photograph: Charles W. Warterfield, Jr.

More generic than the highly personal and highly architected work of Edwin Keeble is a phenomenon known as "builder's classical," in which classical details appear on a purely modern and otherwise architecturally insignificant house form. The portico on a Lebanon Road ranch house (fig. 3.23) is a sensitive use of the Ionic, which nevertheless has little relation to the basically horizontal thrust of the vernacular ranch house. This attenuated form of the classical is present as a generic gesture toward dignified living, a pale reflection of the ideology that found in classicism a national language.

3.21 Residence by Edwin Keeble, interior
Photograph: Susan Adcock

The Classical Echo

The classical style in architecture has had a much longer run than Latin or ancient Greek as a vernacular language. In spite of such relatively recent phenomena as the architectural expressions of so-called post-modern classicism, however, it seems that the appearance of the classical in architecture today bears the same relation to the spoken tongue as a quotation from a poem but dimly remembered.

The classical echoes that we do hear in contemporary Nashville are found not in the city center but in the suburbs. Like the Holly Street Fire Hall of almost a century ago, the

3.22 Residence by Edwin Keeble, interior
Photograph: Susan Adcock

3.23 Classical ranch house, Lebanon Road
Photograph: Charles W. Warterfield, Jr.

120

public buildings placed near our homes today seek an identification with the residential that a classical detail or two can help to promote. Or perhaps such details are a rather desperate allusion to stability and tradition in a modern suburban wilderness that changes almost daily. It is difficult to ascribe motive with certainty, because the echoes we hear are so faint.

The barrel-vaulted false front of a department store in a suburban shopping mall may call to the minds of the initiated the monumental vaults of Roman baths, but for the average drive-by shopper the vault is merely an oversize indicator of entrance (fig. 3.24). The Doric frieze on a Nolensville Road furniture store may have the requisite ornament, but its relation to the building it adorns is as tenuous as the footings of classical civilization on commercial shopping strips (fig. 3.25). The form of a contemporary "big house" on Chickering Road may be a visual metaphor for a broken pediment resting directly on the ground, but it is a metaphor that few would recognize (fig. 3.26).

Today the column and its capital have a vague associative quality rather than a positive ideology. In the nineteenth century, classical styles became gradually detached from their original context and purpose and as a result became accepted by an increasingly industrialized world as decoration. Industrialization demanded an acceptance of new techniques of engineering, but architects of that period missed the opportunity to bring classicism up to date by revising the classical vocabulary to suit the new materials. The twentieth-century architectural and social critic Lewis Mumford describes the post-Civil

3.24 Dillard's department store, Green Hills Mall
Photograph: Charles W. Warterfield, Jr.

121

War state of affairs between architecture and engineering as a disjunction between the dead language of the classics and the living language of the machine. The classical was employed with no inner logic or rationale.

In the present, the classical style whispers to us through vaguely allusive forms, often inappropriately applied. "I can't tell you how many times people attach carriage lamps to Victorian houses, or choose "Colonial" light fixtures for much later downtown historic districts, or place crown moldings in an industrial building, and then say, 'You'll love it; it's historic,'" says Ann Reynolds, executive director of the Metro Nashville Historical Commission.

In spite of such casual appropriations, the classical style has met Nashville's evolving need to be a part of the nation, then to separate from it, and then to be at one with the nation again while maintaining a certain distinctiveness of culture. In Nashville, Andrew Jackson and William Strickland, the Hardings of Belle Meade plantation, and the residents of Belle Meade Boulevard forged from the ethos of classicism a significant part of our local color. It is doubtful

3.25 Commercial building, Nolensville Road
Photograph: Charles W. Warterfield, Jr.

if the classical will ever stage a major architectural comeback here, but the continuing presence of its historic structures in the fabric of our lives is crucial to our understanding of who we were then and who we are now.

3.26 A Small World,
Tuck Hinton Architects,
Chickering Road
Photograph: Charles
W. Warterfield, Jr.

Athena's New Dwelling

The Nashville Parthenon and the Nashville Athena

For Athens alone of her contemporaries is found when tested to be greater than her reputation. . . . The admiration of the present and succeeding ages will be ours, since we have not left our power without witness.

PERICLES

Situated in the heart of one of Nashville's oldest and best-known urban parks stands a concrete Parthenon, the world's only full-scale and detailed replica of antiquity's most famous building. Other than the name Centennial Park, the building is the only public remnant of the state of Tennessee's elaborate celebration marking the centenary of its admission to the Union in 1796. Since it was built, the Parthenon has been a defining emblem of the city of Nashville.

Although Nashville's image since the 1960s has been overlaid with and sometimes obscured by the city's ties to the music industry, the Parthenon is still a prominent symbol. The Chamber of Commerce, for example, used the building as the visual focus of a recent billboard campaign for Nashville in London (fig. 4.1).

Centennial Origins of the Nashville Parthenon

The idea of a Centennial Exposition itself was first proposed in the fall of 1893 by Col. W. C. Smith in the hope that it would stimulate the economy. The entire country was in the midst of a depression and Colonel Smith, in his formal statement to the Commercial Club, proposed an exposition

124

to "divert the attention of our own people, if possible, from the general depression, by setting on foot some enterprise that will interest them especially in behalf of our own State, and that will tend to enlist their aid and cooperation in furthering the interests of the city of Nashville in particular."[1]

Two years later, Maj. E. C. Lewis, who had been elected director general of the Exposition, submitted a plan that included at its center a Fine Arts Building that would be an exact reproduction of the Parthenon.[2] Great attention to detail and to all existing evidence of the original was paid during the initial construction of the replica. In fact, Major Lewis requested and received from King of George I of Greece architectural and archaeological studies, photographs, and drawings.[3] Herman Justi, editor of *The Official History of the Tennessee Centennial Exposition*, recorded of the Nashville Parthenon: "In size, in detail it is believed to be, a recreation of what Ictinus built and Phidias adorned. All the best authorities were carefully studied, and Penrose, whose investigations seem to have been the most thorough, and whose conclusions appear the most probable, was religiously followed by the accomplished architect in charge."[4] Drawings of the original Parthenon made by French diplomat Jacques Carrey in 1674, thirteen years before the explosion

4.1 Billboard, London, England, 1994
Source: Nashville Convention and Visitors Bureau

125

of stored gunpowder that destroyed it, were invaluable in designing the pediments.[5] Since so much of the east pediment was missing by the time Carrey made his drawings, the west pediment figures were reproduced on both ends of the building[6] (fig. 4.2).

According to the resolution adopted by the organizers of the Exposition in 1894, the Fine Arts building was always intended as a permanent structure, to remain when the rest of the buildings were dismantled at the conclusion of the six-month long celebration.[7] The Parthenon as it was constructed for the Centennial, however, had its outer coating and all its sculpture made of an exterior-grade plaster called "staff." Within ten years after the Exposition closed, the sculpture had deteriorated badly and the pediment figures had been removed. Eventually the building posed a safety hazard and the Park Board commissioners, who bore responsibility since the Exposition grounds had become a city park in 1902, decided to rebuild the Parthenon out of a more permanent material.

4.2 The Parthenon, east facade, 1897

Source: Parthenon Collection

The Rebuilding in Permanent Form

The city fathers decided to rebuild in 1920 and selected the architect Russell Hart to draw the plans (fig. 4.3). As the art pavilion for the Centennial, however, the 1897 building was an exterior replica only. The interior was designed as a series of large exhibition spaces for displaying paintings and sculpture from around the world, described as "the most valuable works of art ever exhibited in the South, and one of the best loan collections ever seen in the United States"[8] (fig. 4.4).

The challenge for architect Hart, therefore, was twofold: to design a historically accurate interior from the almost total ruin of the original and to determine the most appropriate building material for this permanent reconstruction. In selecting a building material, Hart had to balance permanence against cost in trying to achieve the look of the original in Greece. Marble was too expensive; plaster had already proved impermanent; reinforced concrete, the most progressive new structural technique, did not look at all like the original. Eventually Hart decided to use concrete, but to cover it with a newly patented concrete aggregate formulated by the John Early Studio in Washington, D.C. (fig. 4.5). This aggregate could be colored to look as much as possible like the weathered Pentelic marble of the original and even allowed for the inclusion of permanent bright blue and brick red as background colors to the sculpture and portions of the decorative trim, as was the case with the original.

To assist in the design of the interior, Hart hired William Bell Dinsmoor as consulting architect. Dinsmoor had done extensive archaeological work in Greece and was considered the foremost author-

4.3 Russell Hart
Source: Parthenon Collection

ity on ancient architecture; his reputation is still unsurpassed. In his definitive work, *The Architecture of Ancient Greece*, Dinsmoor states, "While there are several more or less faithful modern replicas of the exterior of the Parthenon, the only reproduction of the interior at full size is that which I designed in 1927 for the Parthenon in Nashville, Tennessee"[9] (fig. 4.6). The exterior of the Nashville Parthenon was completed in 1925 and the interior in 1931 (fig. 4.7).

The original Parthenon has long been considered the architectural epitome of the golden age of Greece because of the number and subtlety of the architectural refinements used in its construction. The Parthenon is sixty-five feet

*4.4 The Parthenon
interior, 1897*
Source: Parthenon Collection

*4.5 The reconstruction of
the Parthenon, ca. 1921*
Source: Parthenon Collection

128

high at its apex with its superstructure resting on a base consisting of three steps. The top step, or stylobate, the platform on which the columns rest, is 228 feet long by 101 feet wide. Forty-six Doric columns form the colonnaded peristyle, with seventeen columns along each side and eight along each end (the corner columns being counted twice). This number of columns is greater than on a typical Doric temple and corresponds to the increased size of the naos, or enclosed space of a temple, which was designed to accommodate the huge statue of Athena. The columns of the peristyle are thirty-four feet high, including the capital, with an approximate diameter at the base of six feet. They do not taper in a straight line but in a slight convex curve, the widest point of which is only three-quarters of an inch off the straight and occurs about thirteen and a half feet up. This gentle swelling is known as entasis.

The second of the more visible refinements is the curvature of all the horizontal lines of the building. On the long side the steps are four inches higher at the center than at either end, and this rise is included in all the horizontals, from the foundation through the entablature. Finally, all the columns, as well as the interior walls, incline slightly toward the center of the building. Out of plumb by almost three inches, the columns of the sides would meet if extended 6,600 feet into the air; those of the ends would meet at approximately 15,000 feet.

As Susan Woodford says of these major and very subtle refinements in her booklet *The Parthenon*: "Any simple post and lintel structure made out of many identical repeated units is in danger of look-

4.6 The Parthenon interior, ca. 1930

Source: Parthenon collection

ing lifeless and mechanical. Many buildings that imitate the Parthenon do. The architectural refinements are meant to counteract this. They modify just those parts of the temple that otherwise would look most severe and rigid: the straight lines and right angles."[10] The architects and builders of the Nashville Parthenon were careful to study and include in this recreation all the subtleties of the original. If a visitor looks closely, the entasis of the columns, the curvature of the long base, and, less obviously, the inclination of the columns are all visible (fig. 4.8).

The construction of Nashville's permanent Parthenon was a start-stop affair, since work could only move as fast as Hart could complete work drawings and as the Park Board had funds available.[11] By the time the building was opened to the public in May 1931, the United States was well into the Great Depression, and the building, though structurally completed, was without two of its most important features: the enormous statue of Athena, which was the focal point of the original, and the Ionic frieze, a band of low-relief sculpture around the top of the exterior walls under the surrounding colonnade.

4.7 The reconstruction of the Parthenon, 1925

Source: Parthenon Collection

Though technically an incomplete replica, the building was as accurate in detail as current scholarship could make it. The metopes of the original—the sculpted panels that alternate with triglyphs to make up the Doric frieze running around the outer edge of the building just below the roof line—told a different story on each side of the building, but only the south side metopes had survived antiquity sufficiently unharmed to be duplicated. South side metopes are

4.8 View along the south side of the Parthenon, 1948
Photograph by Charles W. Warterfield, Jr.

131

therefore repeated on all four sides of the replica. A complete set of casts of the existing fragments of the pedimental sculptures, known to the world as the Elgin Marbles, was purchased from the British Museum to be used as the basis for casting the figures for Nashville (fig. 4.9).

Temple of the Arts, Home of Athena

Although the Centennial Exposition as a whole had emphasized the state's industrial and technological progress, the Parthenon, in its capacity as Fine Arts Pavilion, was at the heart of the Exposition. In an unpublished paper, Metro Historical Commission Executive Director Ann Reynolds writes: "In contrast to the manufacturing, industrial, and utilitarian character of the North, the South had long seen itself romantically as the heir to the classical legacy of fine arts, even as it sought the wealth of capitalism."[12] This attitude found expression in Nashville and especially in the Centennial itself. Justi observes: "The exaltation of the Parthenon at Nashville was no mere accident. . . . [I]t is the symbol of a great recovery in American life, a reinstatement of Art as the Crown of Commerce."[13]

4.9 Making the pediment sculptures, ca. 1924

Source: Parthenon Collection

The building never completely gave up its identity as a "temple for the arts."[14] During the period between 1898 and 1920, the Nashville Art Association held periodic exhibitions in the Parthenon. During the reconstruction phase, an anonymous donor offered to give the city part of his collection of American paintings to be housed at the Parthenon, if the Park Board would pledge to finish the building and to construct a secure, fireproof gallery for them. James M. Cowan's name was revealed only after his death in 1930, by which time he had given sixty-three paintings. This collection shares space with changing exhibitions on the lower level of the Parthenon. Although the Parthenon of the fifth century B.C. never housed art exhibits, its very structure and ornamentation were paeans to the three-dimensional art forms of sculpture and architecture, and the Propylaea, gateway to the Acropolis, is said by some to have had a wing devoted to painting.

The idea of completing the interior of the replica by re-creating the enormous statue of Athena refused to go away. In the mid-1930s, sculptors Belle Kinney and Leopold Scholz presented the Park Board with a four-foot model of Athena and a proposal to sculpt both the huge statue and the Ionic frieze. Once again the money was unavailable, and the project was dormant for another thirty years. Sometime in the late 1960s a donation box appeared next to Belle Kinney's model in the middle of the Parthenon. School children, visitors, and Nashvillians put their nickels, dimes, and dollar bills in that box over the next twelve years.

In 1982, with $30,000 of seed money from the contribution box, the project to reconstruct Athena Parthenos began. A competition for the commission was announced, to be won by a native Nashvillian, sculptor Alan LeQuire, who was only twenty-six years old at the time. Although LeQuire initially estimated that the project would take eighteen months, it actually took over seven years. LeQuire worked tirelessly, inventing his way through a project that had not been attempted during the intervening 2,500 years. His forty-two foot statue of Athena was unveiled in May 1990, bringing Nashville's tribute to ancient Athens one step closer to a complete and accurate replica.

Significance and Motives, Modern and Ancient

The significance of the Nashville Parthenon to scholars is obvious. It is the only place in the world where one can see the whole Parthenon as the Greeks built it, to get a physical sense of the space and the way in which the statue of Athena filled it, and thereby to gain some understanding in tangible form of the civilization that created it.

But the significance of the replica to Nashvillians is also closely bound to the notion of the city as "Athens of the South." The emphasis the first settlers of the city placed on education and self-government comes to visible fruition with the completion of the Parthenon and its Athena. Along with the rest of the newly-formed nation, the early settlers took as their model the social and political structure of Athens in its golden age. Therefore it is not surprising that, even a hundred years later, the building style for the Exposition as a whole was a nod to the classical.

Since Greek Revival architecture was generally favored for public buildings in the interior South after about 1830,[15] the preference was already well established by the time of the Tennessee Centennial Exposition. That the organizers of the Exposition were conscious of this predilection is apparent from the comments at the time. Writing in the official history, George W. Chambers observed: "South of the Mason-Dixon line this is the architecture that was chosen for the stately homes, as well as for State and public buildings. That choice of the classic Greek for all important work, domestic and national, is distinctly the choice of the South. It would seem that, approaching the parallel of Athens in this country it was a sine qua non to follow its architecture."[16] The choice of a replica of the Parthenon for the centerpiece of the state's centennial celebration, then, was a deliberate reinforcement of Nashville's self-image.

The Exposition itself had both economic and political motives. The historian of the Exposition claims pure patriotism as the overriding motive, "the noble objective of honoring the memories and commemorating the deeds of the pioneers of a great Commonwealth." He then says that other reasons involved were a "desire to advertise and develop the matchless and boundless resources of Tennessee, to increase its population by inviting desirable settlers, and to increase its wealth by tempting foreign capital."[17] In the fall of 1893, writes Justi, "There was an all pervading despondency in the community; the spark of hope was dim in the stoutest heart; the aftermath of the storm was terrible. The gaunt specter of want . . . seemed to perch itself above the rich man's mansions, no less than over the door of the day-laborer."[18]

The Exposition was thus proposed as a way to propel a sluggish economy and to fire the imagination of the citizenry. Referring to Colonel W. C. Smith, who first proposed an Exposition, Justi says, "His purpose was to awaken public spirit, revive the hopes of the people, advertise and develop the matchless resources of the state, renew the memory of its founders, and illustrate the progress of a hundred years."[19]

Pericles' building program on the Acropolis, which began with the Parthenon in 447 B.C., had a similar mix of motives. Pericles was also faced with the aftermath of a debilitating war, in his case the war against the Persians. Construction on the scale of his plans for the Acropolis required skilled artisans by the hundreds and unskilled laborers by the thousands, all of whom were paid.

The need to proclaim the greatness and progress of Athens as a society also underlay the building program on the Acropolis. The Athenians of the fifth century B.C., especially those of the philosophical bent of Pericles, thought of themselves as representative of the forces of civilization: intellectual, pure, progressive, and just, constantly at war with the opposing forces of barbarism and chaos.

The sculptural ornamentation of the Parthenon and the Athena refers to this conflict through mythological battles, in each case Greek against outsiders: Theseus against the Amazons, Lapiths against the Centaurs, and heroic warriors against the giants. As Jeffrey M. Hurwit observes: "The fifth-century Athenian (like Greeks in general) constructed the world in terms of polarities or oppositions—culture and nature, human and animal, rational and irrational, Greek and barbarian, and so on—in which the first terms of every pair (culture, human, rational, Greek) constituted the norm and the ideal. In such an intellectual context, it is not surprising that the imagery of the Parthenon addressed many of these antitheses." The victory of Theseus over the Amazons, found on Athena's shield and on the west side metopes, Hurwit notes, is "the victory of civilization over barbarity and disorder, of West over East, of Greece over Persia."[20]

There is thus a strong element of self-congratulation in the elaborate group of buildings the people of Athens designed and built under Pericles' leadership. Probably the organizers of the Tennessee Centennial Exposition were not conscious of mirroring their Athenian predecessors so closely.

4.10 The Parthenon, south side, 1990

Photograph: Gary Layda

In 1989, Paul Goldberger, architecture critic for the *New York Times,* commented, "In 1897 [the Parthenon] was nothing but a copy, although it was a copy built by people who

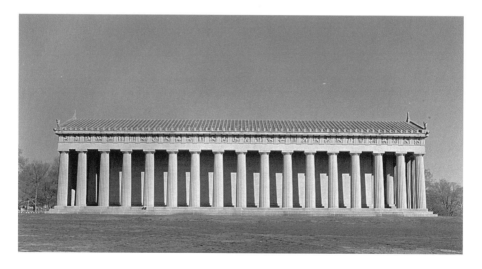

very much wanted it to represent Nashville as well as Athens. And in time it did just that: such is its power as a work of architecture that it has transcended its origins and become, in effect, a symbol not only of copying Greece but of Nashville's own identity as a place."[21] By continuing the work of completing the replica, both in the 1920s and more recently with the recreation of Athena, Nashville reconfirms her conscious identification with the best of ancient Athens.

The Athena Parthenos in antiquity was a civic deity. The Athenians believed that she ensured the progress, prosperity, and health of their city. To her they owed their recent victory over the Persians. She was wisdom incarnate and she was the patron of all the useful arts, such as weaving and pottery.

In Nashville, Athena symbolizes a society that respects art, education, and democracy. The Parthenon epitomizes classical Nashville and translates into physical form the attributes so admired in ancient Athens. As the designers of the original Parthenon self-consciously placed Athens firmly on one side of the everlasting struggle between civilization and barbarism, so the builders of the Parthenon replica, in each generation, self-consciously place Nashville squarely in the tradition represented by Athens: progressive, self-governing, respectful of the arts, championing truth and enlightenment (fig. 4.10).

Alan LeQuire's odyssey to discover, capture, and re-create the essence of the Athena Parthenos is the fulfillment of the Parthenon as a symbol of Nashville.

Athena Parthenos
The Re-creation in Nashville
Alan LeQuire

The story behind the Nashville Athena is a seven-and-one-half year history of cooperation among many people. Few realize that the statue was not funded by the city of Nashville but rather almost entirely by small donations from individuals. Engineers and architects as well as my assistants and friends donated their labor. Archaeological scholars shared their research and advice. Business owners contributed materials and equipment. The Parks Department personnel allowed the project to continue despite delays and setbacks. Through the many difficult obstacles, Anne F. Roos gave the project direction, and our success is due primarily to her guidance.

Because the re-creation of Athena Parthenos involved so many people, and because the statue itself contains so much cultural and historical information, there are a variety of ways to approach it. Athena can be seen as a document in the history of religion, or simply as a modern construction pro-

4.11 Alan LeQuire's
Athena Parthenos, 1990
Photograph: Dana Thomas

ject. She can be seen as the result of a unique public art fund-raising event, or as a revitalization of mythological symbolism. One can even view the entire process as a long conceptual piece, or as a seven-and-one-half year performance. In any case the statue provides a wealth of information to the interested learner.

Not being an archaeologist, I had to rely on the work of others. In November 1982, I was fortunate to have been supplied with *Athena Parthenos, a Reconstruction* by Neda Leipen. As curator of the Greek and Roman department of the Royal Ontario Museum, Neda Leipen compiled and evaluated the statue's literary and three-dimensional evidence, and she helped to construct a model on the scale of approximately 1:10. Her reconstruction and the research behind it became the foundation for my own work. Throughout the project I turned to her monograph for an authoritative archaeological guide.

In 1982, armed with Leipen's monograph and some letters of introduction, I set out for Greece. In Athens, I met the late Professor George Mylonas. Mylonas, who is best known for his work at Mycenae, was then president of the Greek Archaeological Society. His was the first reaction I received from an archaeologist. He was amused, I think, that anyone would take on such a task and was skeptical to say the least. Nevertheless he saw to it that I was allowed into the Parthenon to view the site of the original statue. Moving through that setting and standing in the original space, next to the hole in the floor that held the original wooden support beam, gave me my first sense of *Athena's* reality.

Later I visited the National Museum to view the Roman versions of the statue. The Varvakion, although it is the most complete copy, did not impress me. Among its weaknesses, in my view, is the use of a column to support Athena's right hand. I was biased against the column for aesthetic reasons. The column would look out of place against the background of the Parthenon interior because it would be different in size and style from the surrounding colonnade. It would seem even more incongruous placed atop the base of the statue. Stylistically the Varvakion owes nothing to the classical period, and I knew it could serve me only as an inventory of various details of the statue.

The Varvakion's major stylistic fault is in the stance, specifically, the awkward positioning of the legs. Even with my limited background in art history, I knew that Greek sculptors had mastered the principle of weight-shift well before the classical period. When a figure is at rest (with its weight on one leg) the ankle of the weight-bearing leg, because of the physical properties of the human body, will always fall directly underneath the neck. For a sculptor this is one of the first principles of figure construction, and it is immediately apparent when working from life. The original *Parthenos* must have been in this position because she is portrayed in all the replicas with her left heel raised, indicating that that leg bears no weight. I felt I had to attribute the awkwardness of the stance of the Varvakion to the inexperience of the copyist and not to any defect of the original. The more I investigated this problem, the more convinced I became that the *Parthenos* would have been in the weight-shift position. Figures shown standing at rest in the frieze exhibit the proper placement on the weight-bearing leg, as do other authentic works of the period. This is not the full-blown contrapposto position that we know from Renaissance sculpture, but a limited, more formal weight-shift. The folds of the draping peplos fall vertically from the extended, weight-bearing hip, adding to the columnar solidity of the figure. This is the key to the graceful stance of the Karyatids from the Erechtheion that undoubtedly were influenced by the *Parthenos*. At the British Museum I dropped a plumb line in front of Karyatid "C" just to confirm the fact that the foot falls directly underneath the chin.

The lively qualities of the Lenormant statuette of Athena, another Roman copy, in the National Museum in Athens, impressed me greatly, even though it is a small, unfinished marble carving. But one notable aspect of the statuette is that

4.12 Varvakion statuette, National Museum, Athens

Photograph: Alan LeQuire

the marble has been carefully chipped away on the under side of the right hand, suggesting that the Lenormant sculptor never intended to place a support column beneath it. This observation helped confirm a suspicion of mine that the column might not have been part of Pheidias's original.

One might argue in favor of the column out of a desire to see a more symmetrically balanced composition; however, such a desire for symmetry is probably a modern phenomenon. Because no mention of a column is made in the literary evidence, I chose to leave it out. Such support pieces were, after all, primarily conventional devices of Roman copyists and necessary only when working in marble. I finally became convinced that the column was not part of the original statue once I understood that the cantilever occurs within the figure.

The Varvakion statuette creates a problem in understanding the mechanics of the right arm because the arm is placed forward, necessarily confined to the dimensions of the marble block. In the original statue there would have been no such confinement, and the arm would have extended out at a wider, more natural angle from the body. Besides improving the total composition, this position allows a cantilevered beam to pass through the arm and into the body of the statue. A wooden beam, with or without iron gusseting, could easily bear the weight of Nike, since one end would intersect the central support beam. The fulcrum thus occurs at the elbow and is easily masked by the edge of the chiton.

These two conclusions about the stance and the column were the most important results of my trip to Athens. Before returning to Nashville I stopped in New York to meet Professor Evelyn Harrison and in Bryn Mawr to meet Professor Brunilde Ridgway. Thereafter, these two distinguished archaeological scholars have taken an active interest in my reconstruction.

In my studio I began by working from a human model. I was determined that my statue would have the restrained naturalism that was Pheidias's genius. This resulted in a 1:10

scale version based solely on human proportions, which I transcribed numerically. The next step was to make a larger 1:5 scale model in which the proportions followed those of fifth-century B.C. sculpture. Because this was the piece that I would enlarge to full size, it had to be accurate. Here I was helped again by Professor Ridgway, who was kind enough to visit my studio. She made some suggestions to help improve the authenticity of my model, but where there was room for disagreement, she allowed me that room. I am grateful to her for sharing her knowledge of ancient sculpture, but also for allowing me the freedom to draw my own conclusions.

I made certain perspective distortions in the 1:5 scale model, fully believing that Pheidias would have done the same. Distortions make the enlarged proportions look natural from the ground. Generally speaking, they involve a gradual expansion of measurements according to the distance from the viewer. In addition, certain angles are exaggerated to make them more visible—for example, the position of the eyes. There is ample evidence that such perspective distortions were common in the fifth century, B.C., as can be observed in some of the pedimental sculpture from the temple of Poseidon at Sounion and in that of the temple of Zeus at Olympia.

Prior to working out all the proportions, I had decided to follow William Bell Dinsmoor's suggestion for the total height of the statue. Dinsmoor, a noted architectural historian, provided the authoritative analysis of the Parthenon in *The Architecture of Ancient Greece*, and he assisted with the design and construction of the Nashville Parthenon. I obtained a copy of a drawing from the 1920s that had his profile sketch of Athena in the naos. I therefore felt I was continuing the work he began. Dinsmoor arrived at a figure of 12.73 meters or 41 feet, 10 inches. This is only about 14 inches below the bottom of the wooden ceiling beams of the reconstructed Parthenon. A shorter measurement, while conforming better to modern taste, would not necessarily be in keeping with the purpose of the Doric temple, which, as

Sir Herbert Read reminds us, is meant to shelter an image of a god with just space enough for that image and for an altar.

As the construction of the statue progressed, the proportions of the figure were confirmed by the proportions of the architecture. The right hand, for instance, falls at the same level as the interior architrave. In addition, when viewed from the east door, the helmet and head of the statue rise above the lines of the upper architrave and ceiling beams. *Athena* completely fills the space with which her proportions are in harmony.

The decisions I made during construction of the 1:5 scale model were only the beginning. Enlarging and casting took about three years. By the fall of 1987 I had assembled the body of the statue, but I realized that the work was only about half finished. What remained was to sculpt, cast, and assemble the helmet with its griffins, pegasoi, and sphinx, the forearms, the six-foot-four Nike, the fifteen-foot shield with its thirty-one figures in relief, and the twenty-one figures on the base, not to mention a thirty-foot serpent with thousands of individual scales. Again I followed the advice and research of Brunilde Ridgway and Evelyn Harrison. The Amazonomachy on the shield is based on Professor Harrison's reconstruction, and Professor Ridgway was particularly helpful with Nike and the helmet. The relief on the base is partly derived from Neda Leipen's reconstruction, with certain alterations of figure placement based on Professor Harrison's and my own opinions. I felt I had some freedom with the base composition, since there is little surviving evidence for it.

The results of my archaeological research in 1982 are by no means faultless. Although I tried to eliminate my modern prejudices and my own style, one of the lessons I learned is that such an attempt is futile when there is no original to follow. Inevitably my style and personality come through in the work. I gradually accepted this fact, trusting that in the end my personal inclinations might bear some resemblance to the style of Pheidias.

In 1989, as the statue neared completion, the tragic massacre in China's Tianenmen Square made me realize the significance of *Athena* for the many Nashvillians who helped to build her. She is our Lady Liberty, a living symbol of justice and democracy. In this way she has taken on more significance than I ever anticipated.

By completing *Athena* I am continuing a celebration begun in Tennessee in 1896. Besides being a civic event, *Athena* is also a glorification of the Greek ability to animate the inanimate—to enliven matter. This is the central mystery of sculpture, one that occurs in that moment when a piece of clay, stone, or plaster takes on life. The Parthenon is a monument both abstract and organic that illustrates this mystery inside and out. The entasis or swelling of each column suggests life, as does the curving surface of stylobate. This principle is carried through in the lines of the entire building, suggesting a roundness within, a seed or kernel within the form. With the completion of the statue we have placed the kernel in the shell and have given spirit to the monument.

Classical Continuities

The art of free society consists, first,
in the maintenance of the symbolic code; and,
secondly, in fearlessness of revision.

ALFRED NORTH WHITEHEAD

There are ghosts on the north slope of Nashville's Capitol Hill. They are not the vaporous apparitions that visit on certain midnights but solid Tennessee limestone ghosts, carved from the earth and now slowly subsiding back into it. They are some of the original columns and capitals of the State Capitol, and their message has to do with time.

These fragments of our classical heritage no longer stand in geometric symmetry. They lie in pieces, seemingly at random, and show the scars and shaling of severe weathering. The fluted columns with their striations suggest the history of the planet itself. As rough to the touch as a cat's tongue, they have the feel of time, grainy and dissolute.

These pieces of our past are not the stuff of archaeology in the Old World sense. Quarried locally after construction on the Capitol began in 1845, these columns embodied Tennessee's dream of a golden age to rival that of ancient Greece. The United States was barely seventy years old, Nashville little more than fifty, and we needed an infusion of history.

In 1955 it was discovered that the hundred-year-old exterior of the Capitol was coming apart. The Tennessee lime-

145

stone had weathered poorly, so both the columns and the cornices were pulled off and replicated in Indiana limestone. The original pieces were piled on a hill near the old Tennessee State Penitentiary, where they waited for some new significance.

That significance came in time, some forty years later. Today some of the fragments have been placed on the north flank of Capitol Hill, in their own memorial garden, as a tribute to the stone carvers who worked so diligently under William Strickland to bring the glory of Greek classicism to the frontier (fig. Conclusion 1). They are a small-scale version of the ancient tradition of ruins of remembrance. In 480 B.C. Athens, invading Persians leveled the partially completed temple of Athena and other monuments that stood on the Acropolis. The attackers destroyed not only the buildings but also the sense of sanctuary for which the site stood. When Pericles began to build his Parthenon in 447 B.C., parts of the remains were used to pave and shore up the surrounding hill. The pieces were left visible in the north side of the cliff as a reminder to all Athenians of what had been lost yet also retained. For the Greeks, both present devotions and past history were the stuff of sacrament.

The Strickland fragments similarly bind the past to the present on Nashville's acropolis. They lie in their own garden as part of the restoration and renovation of Capitol Hill that includes, immediately adjacent, a belvedere overlooking Tennessee's monument to its two-hundredth year: the Bicentennial Mall.

Taken in conjunction, the old columns and the new mall articulate in three dimensions the past, present, and future of the classical style in Nashville.

Conclusion 1. Tribute to the Stone Carvers, Capitol Hill

Photograph: Charles W. Warterfield, Jr.

The time-blurred columns of Strickland silently prophesy the inevitable passing of all that is man-made: Delphi or Pompeii, Athens or Nashville. That Tennessee at two hundred has fashioned a memorial with this oracular message establishes a continuity with the classical past that reaches beyond the New World of the nineteenth century to the ancient ruins of the Mediterranean.

The Bicentennial Mall expands the classical spirit into Nashville's present and future. While the Mall is a state rather than a city project, as was the Centennial Exposition of a hundred years earlier, it represents some ancient Athenian ideals in contemporary forms. Tradition requires constant reinterpretation to remain alive.[1]

The Bicentennial Mall

The widely felt need to preserve our classical tradition stimulated the planning impetus behind Tennessee's Bicentennial Mall. As early as the turn of the century, concern had surfaced among Nashvillians over the gradual loss of visual dominance by Strickland's Capitol. With the addition of skyscrapers to the skyline, beginning in the 1950s, that concern became acute. The large plain of land to the north became the sole means available to infuse some stamina into the visual presence of the city's most important historic structure. Governor Ned McWherter and the Bicentennial Commission decided on the Mall as a fitting way to celebrate the state's birthday by preserving a strong sightline to the state's classical incarnation (fig. Conclusion 2a).

Classical principles of order, symmetry, and clarity are embodied in the Mall by means of a ground plan that filters these ideals through the practices of Renaissance and Baroque planning. A nineteen-acre rectangle, the Mall is bordered on the west by the history walk, a Tennessee time line divided into decades by a linear procession of pylons that recall the roofless columns of ancient ruins. The eastern edge is formed by a path that undulates in a representation of the state's topography as it climbs from the Mississippi

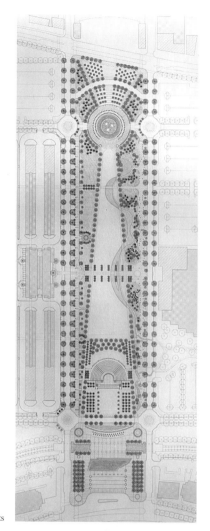

*Conclusion 2a. Drawing
of Bicentennial Mall,
north at top*
Source: Tuck Hinton Architects

*Conclusion 2b. Open-air
theater, with Capitol in
background, looking south*
Photograph: Charles W.
Warterfield, Jr.

148

floodplains to the mountains of the east. Within these borders, paths laid out in diagonals of diminishing perspective worthy of a Renaissance painting lead to the northern end of the Mall and to a carillon enclosing 280 degrees of a circle that relays the focus back to Strickland's Capitol.

Another element of the Mall that brings focus to the Capitol is a literal revival of a classical motif. An open-air theater, composed of concrete risers and grass terraces, is situated in a partially excavated site to replicate the earthen compass of the Greek theater. It faces to the south so that the Capitol forms a backdrop for performances (see fig. Conclusion 2b). The scene is powerfully reminiscent of ancient Athens, where the Theater of Dionysos was similarly situated on the slopes of the Acropolis beneath a colonnaded temple.

As a massive public works project undertaken not for a strictly functional purpose but for the education and delight of the citizens, the Mall is a late revival of the City Beautiful Movement, which brought a classically inspired civic purpose to the planning of pre-World War I American cities. As a memorial to the unique heritage and character of the Volunteer State, the Mall recalls the Acropolis of Athens and the Forum of Rome, among many ancient sites that used civic financial resources for purposes of collective gathering, commemoration, and ceremony. A public space dedicated to education, aesthetic delight, and civic identity, Tennnessee's Bicentennial Mall distills the essence of classicism in many of the same ways that the Parthenon did in Centennial Park a hundred years earlier.

The Parthenon at One Hundred

The rebuilding in permanent form of the Parthenon in the 1920s and 1930s proved to be not quite so permanent after all. Although the building is still structurally sound, the decorative work on the roof and the pedimental sculptures have suffered because of the building methods employed at the time.

John Earley's use of concrete reinforced with steel rods,

not only for the roof tiles and ornamentation but also for the sculptures themselves, was forward-looking at the time he undertook the work. The rods were not stainless steel, however, and very often they were close to the surfaces of the decorations. Because concrete is porous, in time the reinforcing rods have rusted, escalating the deterioration of the concrete.

The restoration work on the exterior has been complicated by several factors. One is that the Potomac River gravel, used for the aggregate to approximate the color value of the original's Pentelic marble, can no longer be dredged, for environmental reasons. Further, no "as built" plans have been found for the final building. When architect Russell Hart's drawings were adapted to on-site realities, no detailed changes were recorded. The absence of those records and specifications have hampered the design of repairs and replacements for elements.

Gradually these problems are being solved by sophisticated methods of back-formulation of Earley's composition and by the discovery of alternate sources for the required materials. Gresham, Smith & Partners began the exterior renovation process in 1992, with David Evans of Ann Arbor, Michigan, as consulting architect. The total estimated cost of replacing only the roof and eaves, together with their decorative features, is some $3,000,000. Repair or replacement of the pedimental sculptures is still in the future.

Nevertheless, more than a quarter-million visitors stream through the Parthenon each year, and its educational programs are more extensive than ever. In addition to staff-led guided lectures and tours, the Parthenon offers teacher packets for school groups, an annual series of lectures called the Parthenon Symposia, and musical concerts each fall—all free to the public. Film and video crews also find the historic building a desirable location.

The story of two artists, brother and sister, illustrates the impact the Parthenon can have on those who live near it. Jim Cogswell, a member of the art faculty at the University of

Michigan, and Margaret Cogswell, a New York sculptor, moved to Nashville as young teenagers. "I remember wandering through [the Parthenon] as a kid," Jim Cogswell recalls, "before any restoration was done. And in the sixth grade, I became very interested in Greek mythology. . . . For all I knew, every city had a Parthenon."[2]

Margaret Cogswell compares the importance of the Parthenon to Nashville with that of the Eiffel Tower to Paris. Both attract meaning "like lightening rods attract thunderbolts." Margaret adds, "The Parthenon has always been a looming form, a curious presence in my life as a young girl in Nashville.

In July 1995, the two artists installed a site-specific exhibition in the Parthenon, inspired by the many facets of the city. Music recordings were used in some of the pieces. Books representing the city's tradition of learning and publishing were wrapped around ears of corn, the food staple of the original Native American inhabitants. The installation also featured woodblock prints of a striding Athena in full regalia printed over maps of Nashville. "The show," said Jim Cogswell at the time of its installation, "is a celebration of something that is unique to Nashville. It's about being in Nashville and being in the Parthenon. It couldn't take place anywhere else."

Most of all, with the re-creation of the monumental Athena in the Nashville Parthenon, the hundredth anniversary of that remarkable building takes on added significance. As the city nears the turn of the millennium, Nashvillians still have close at hand, as they did from the beginning, the promises Athena granted to ancient Athens: education and the arts in a peaceful city that nurtures all its citizens.

Education, the Arts, and Public Life

The continuity of the classical tradition in education, theater, and the arts is surprisingly vital in Nashville at the end of the twentieth century.

At Montgomery Bell Academy, a stalwart commitment to

151

classical education continues to the present day. The curriculum offers classical Greek, and two years of Latin are still required for all students, with four as an option. Living proof of this commitment, two hundred and fifty MBA students took the 1995 National Latin Examination; two hundred received commendations, and ten earned perfect scores on their respective examinations.

Latin in Nashville is not the sole preserve of the private academies. In 1995–96 the public school system of Metropolitan Nashville boasted a total of thirteen teachers of Latin. Latin programs exist not only in each of the city's high schools but now in three middle schools as well. In addition, Latin is offered to sixth-graders in one of the programs for talented students based at Robertson Academy—a school named, appropriately, for the founder of Nashville who was so strongly committed to education.

In the spring of 1994, approximately twelve hundred Latin students from all over the state gathered at Overton High School for the state convention of the Junior Classical League. Dressed in classical garb for the entire weekend, they competed in academic tests, costume contests, declamation events, and even athletic competitions.

At the college and university level, Latin is part of the curriculum at Aquinas Junior College and Belmont University. After suffering a decline following World War II,[3] the Department of Classical Studies at Vanderbilt was re-established under the leadership H. Lloyd Stow, a University of Chicago Ph.D. who was brought to Vanderbilt by Chancellor Harvey Branscomb in 1952. Since that time the program has continued to expand. Classical civilization courses are offered on a wide range of subjects, and Latin and Greek may be pursued through the Ph.D. level. Classics faculty on both the secondary and university level participate actively in the Tennessee Classical Association, composed of Latin teachers and faculty members from all parts of the state.

Other activities, too, attest to the vitality of the classical tradition. Every year since 1980, students at Vanderbilt have competed in the Bernstein Competition in Latin Declamation, an event endowed by a classics graduate in honor of his father, also a classics graduate of Vanderbilt. Eta Sigma Phi, the national classics honorary society for university classics majors, awards medals to outstanding students of Latin in the public and private schools of Nashville. Beginning in 1984, the university reinstituted a biennial Vanderbilt Latin Day for area high school students and their teachers, during which faculty members offer seminars on topics of general interest. This event restores a tradition going back to the 1930s and 1940s, in which Latin students from all over the state came to Vanderbilt to participate in academic competitions.

Not all of the continuities of the classics take place in the classroom. Initiated in 1983 with sponsorship by the Metro Nashville Board of Parks and Recreation, Theatre Parthenos began sponsoring productions of ancient Greek dramas in English translation, presented outdoors on the steps of the Parthenon. Having become an independent arts organization with its own board of directors, Theatre Parthenos has presented such plays as *Oedipus the King*, *Medea*, *Antigone*, *The Oresteia*, *The Trojan Women*, Aristophanes' comedy *Roasting Euripides (Thesmophoriazusae)*, and *The Bacchae* (fig. Conclusion 3). In the spirit of ancient Athens, where a special public fund was maintained to provide the cost of a theater ticket for those who could not afford one, these performances were free to all citizens in the community.

After the 1990 season, the

Conclusion 3. Theatre Parthenos production of Medea

Source: Parthenon Collection

productions of Theatre Parthenos were temporarily suspended due to the exterior restorations of the Parthenon and the need to secure directorial leadership and corporate or public funding. The impact, however, continues. A parent taking a group of inner-city fourth-graders on a field trip tells of entertaining her young passengers en route with stories from Greek mythology. When she came to the end of the encounter of Odysseus with the Cyclops, one of the children asked, "Tell us the story about the two brothers who killed each other and the king wouldn't let their sisters bury one of them." "How did you know the story of Antigone?" asked the parent. "My parents took me to a play in Centennial Park," said the child.

Some remnants of Nashville's classical past resonate mostly as echoes, albeit with a distinctive tone. The historical commitments of Roger Williams University and Fisk University to liberal education, for example, extend into the present in the person of John Hope Franklin. Franklin's parents, Buck Colbert Franklin and Mollie Lee Parker Franklin, both attended Roger Williams University in the late 1890's. Buck Colbert Franklin studied Latin and Greek with a Dr. Truesdale and also with John Hope, a professor recently arrived from Brown University who became a lifelong friend of the couple. Buck and Mollie Franklin's second son, John Hope Franklin, recalls as a young child watching his father read Greek.[4]

John Hope Franklin, after a distinguished career at the University of Chicago, is John B. Duke Professor of History Emeritus at Duke University, a former president of the American Historical Association, and a 1995 recipient of the Presidential Medal of Freedom. Franklin brought two years of Latin with him to Fisk University, where he was a 1935 honor graduate of Fisk University and where he served as a long-time member of the Board of Trust. At Fisk he took two years each of German and French at the urging of his mentor, Theodore Currier, in preparation for graduate study at Harvard University, although Latin was still an option. In writing of the wide array of educational institutions in Nashville, Franklin observes that some of them had achieved national reputation and influence. "Thus," he concludes, "Nashville was not only the Athens of the South but the mecca for so many who sought to raise their own educational and intellectual sights."[5]

Another distinguished Fisk graduate, Wade McCree of the class of 1941, served as a federal judge and later as U.S. Solicitor General. When one of the authors of this volume met him at a Fisk event in 1969, McCree smiled when he learned of her interests in classics and proceeded to quote the first lines of the *Iliad* in Greek.

Other classical continuities are embodied in present-day Nashvillians. State Senator Douglas Henry fondly recounts his two years of Latin with Mr. Wallace at the Wallace University School. When the Wallace School closed, Henry went to Chattanooga to complete high school at the McCauley School. While there, he studied Cicero and Vergil and car-

Conclusion 4.
First Inauguration of Nashville Mayor Phil Bredesen, in front of the Parthenon, September 16, 1991.

Photograph: Gary Layda

ried on an active correspondence with Mr. Wallace in Latin. A mayoral inauguration was held in front of the Parthenon, emphasizing the civic nature of the site (fig. Conclusion 4).

Philip Lindsley's great-granddaughter Margaret Lindsley Warden was prominent among those Nashvillians celebrating the state's bicentennial in 1996. A writer and historian, Margaret Lindsley Warden proudly shows visitors her larger-than-lifesize bust of the Roman poet Vergil—a visible symbol of her family's long link with the classical past.

Classics For Whom?

Are the survivals of classical culture in Nashville the private preserve of an elite group of intellectuals, or can the larger community of citizens and visitors, shopkeepers and politicians, executives and laborers, teachers and schoolchildren claim that culture as their own? Fugitive poet Donald Davidson clearly preferred the former view, as his poem on the Parthenon reveals:

ON A REPLICA OF THE PARTHENON

Why do they come? What do they seek
Who build but never read their Greek?
The classic stillness of a pool
Beleaguered in its certitude
By aimless motors that can make
Only incertainty more sure;
And where the willows crowd the pure
Expanse of clouds and blue that stood
Around the gables Athens wrought
Shop-girls embrace a plaster thought,
And eye Poseidon's loins ungirt,
And never heed the brandished spear
Or feel that bright-eyed maiden's rage
Whose gaze the sparrows violate;
But the sky drips its spectral dirt,
And gods, like men, to soot revert.

Gone is the mild, the serene air.
The golden years are come too late.
Pursue not wisdom or virtue here,
But what blind notion, what dim last
Regret of men who slew their past
Raised up this bribe against their fate.[6]

Davidson's discontent with the modern world and the industrial drive that fuels it is distilled with bitter irony in this poem. Critics T. Daniel Young and Thomas Inge observe that Davidson sees the replica of the Parthenon as "an absurd example of the modern misconception of the function of art that is held by a people who desperately attempt to cling to the form but who have not the remotest conception of a classical civilization." They conclude: "The construction of the accurate reproduction is the feeble gesture of a people whose artistic sensibilities have atrophied under the dehumanizing demands of an industrial community."[7]

A Vanderbilt sociologist has argued more recently that what he calls the "Athens idea" has outlived its usefulness and should be left behind. Richard Peterson identifies the "Athens idea" with cultural elitism and academic criticism rather than active creativity and expression. In proposing a rival view, Peterson urges attention to public, not simply private concerns; the broad availability of the arts and aesthetic education; an evolving rather than tradition-bound sense of art and culture; and a cosmopolitan attitude.[8]

Yet we contend that these are the very civic, populist instincts that the classical tradition has long nurtured in Nashville. The power of tradition is amplified when it undergoes constant revision. The danger lies in living with no traditions at all. Allen Tate once wrote that abstraction is the death of religion no less than the death of anything else.[9] We come to understand our experience, he would argue, not by resorting to abstractions, which so easily become rigid ideologies, but by connecting one experience with another.

We need stories larger than our own in order not to wander as orphans in a chilly universe. Some of these stories come from the distant past, but in order for them to nurture us, we must revise and adapt them to our experience in contemporary times.

Further, part of the Athenian ideal is a broad-based civic participation through which the city encourages learning, self-governance, and friendly exchange among its people. African-American activist Barbara Mann, at the time a member of the Metro Nashville Board of Education, spoke to this issue in 1980, on the occasion of the city's two-hundredth anniversary, as she reflected on why she and her husband chose to settle in Nashville:

> *The choice was a deliberate one. My husband and I arrived at the decision about twenty-two years ago to adopt Nashville. We weighed the good and the bad. . . . But there was a quality about Nashville—a part of its character, if you will—that caused us to reject the traditional migration northward. One component of that quality seemed to be a sense of freedom, generated, perhaps, by the Nashville theme—Athens of the South. The existence of so many educational institutions gave encouragement to and support for questioning existing social practices and seeking out solutions for them.*[10]

The classical tradition in Nashville has a past as complex and multifaceted as the city's history. It seems appropriate that a re-creation of Athena presides over the Parthenon, given her many-sided nature.

In Homer's *Odyssey,* Athena was the special guide and companion of Odysseus. Kimon Friar describes the complex and even contradictory character of Odysseus as one who was "modest yet boastful, cunning yet straightforward, heavy-handed yet gentle, affectionate yet harsh, aristocratic yet public-spirited, sensual yet ascetic." Then Friar concludes:

Only one of the twelve Olympian deities had a character equally complex—she who in Homer was Odysseus's constant companion

158

and protector, and for whom the Athenians named their city as a tribute to both their involved temperaments: Athena.[11]

As Nashville's classical symbol, Athena has lent to the city some of her paradoxical nature. Respect for tradition is balanced by an equal respect for innovation that distinguishes Nashville from its eastern seaboard sisters. Here the vigor of the frontier still quickens the pace of this town-turned-metropolis.

Nashville brought Latin and Greek, column and capital to the frontier, and classical currents run deep within the stream of the city's history. These currents continue to move in ways that bring people together and sustain our hopes for both preservation and revision. For all these reasons, Nashville can appropriately claim classical Athens as both an inspiration from the past and a guide for the future.

NOTES

BIBLIOGRAPHY

ABOUT THE AUTHORS

INDEX

Notes

INTRODUCTION

1. Alfred Leland Crabb, *Nashville: Personality of a City* (Indianapolis: Bobbs-Merrill, 1960), 170. Crabb is followed by Louise Davis in an article on the Parthenon in the *Tennessean,* September 26, 1988. Henry McRaven, in *Nashville, "Athens of the South"* (Chapel Hill, N.C.: Scheer & Jervis, 1949), vii, more cautiously states that the "exact origin of the expression is lost in the obscurity of the past." On p. 50, however, he adds, "Dr. Lindsley is generaly [*sic*] credited with originating the phrase "Nashville, Athens of the South."

2. Leroy J. Halsey, *A Sketch of the Life and Educational Labors of Philip Lindsley, D.D.* (Hartford: Williams, Wiley & Turner, 1859; reprinted from *Barnard's American Journal of Education*, September 1859), 41. Halsey (1786–1855) was graduated from the University of Nashville in 1834 and later edited a three-volume edition of Lindsley's lectures and papers, *The Works of Philip Lindsley* (Philadelphia: J. B. Lippincott, 1866).

3. S. Buckingham, quoted in James Patrick, *Architecture in Tennessee 1768–1897* (Knoxville: University of Tennessee Press, 1981), 121.

4. John Egerton, "Athens of the West? A Little culture went a long way in creating image," *Society of Professional Journalists,* 1994 Convention, 11.

CHAPTER I

1. Jesse Wills, "Remembrances," in *Nashville and Other Poems* (Nashville: Fantasie, 1973), 58.

2. G. M. Ramsey, *The Annals of Tennessee to the End of the Eighteenth Century* (1853; reprint, Kingsport, Tenn.: Kingsport, 1926), 657.

3. *Constitution of the State of Tennessee* (Nashville, Division of Publications, Department of State, 1982).

4. [Charles Lester], *The Life of General Sam Houston* (New York, 1855), 21, 22. When Sam Houston was being mentioned as a possible candidate for the U.S. presidency in 1855, as a Southerner with strong Unionist tendencies, an anonymous life was published under the title *The Life of General Sam Houston; the Only Authentic Memoir of Him Ever Published.* That *Life* is identical with few variations to an earlier *Sam Houston and His Republic*, published in 1846. In his 1883 biography of Houston, *Life and Achievements of Sam Houston, Hero and Statesman* (New York, 1883), Charles Lester claimed authorship of both earlier pieces. Since Lester had worked closely with Houston for three months and much of the material was taken verbatim by dictation, we can be fairly confident of the general authenticity of the data in all three works. See Susan Ford Wiltshire, "Sam Houston and the *Iliad, Tennessee Historical Quarterly* 32, no. 9 (fall 1973): 249–254.

5. William Carey Crane, *Life and Select Literary Remains of Sam Houston of*

Texas (Philadelphia: J. B. Lippincott, 1884), 18.

6. Robert Penn Warren, *How Texas Won her Freedom: The Story of Sam Houston and the Battle of San Jacinto* (San Jacinto Monument, Tex.: San Jacinto Museum of History, 1959), 2.

7. Henry McRaven, *Nashville: Athens of the South* (Chapel Hill, N.C.: Scheer & Jervis, 1949), 56.

8. Llerena Friend, "Sam Houston—Bio-bibliographical," *Texas Grand Lodge Magazine* (March 1957): 114.

9. John Donelson's journal is included in *Three Pioneer Tennessee Documents* (Nashville: Tennessee Historical Commission, 1964), 2.

10. William E. Beard, *First Presbyterian Church of Nashville: 100 Years of Service* (Nashville: Foster & Parkes, 1915), 47.

11. Washington College in Lexington, Virginia; Dickinson College; the University of Alabama at Tuscaloosa (twice); South Alabama College at Marion; College of Louisiana at Jackson; and Transylvania. He also turned down the provostship, equivalent to the presidency, of the University of Pennsylvania.

12. John Wooldridge, ed., *History of Nashville, Tenn.* (Nashville: Publishing House of the Methodist Episcopal Church South, 1890), 618.

13. We are indebted to the research of Robert A. McGaw on the history of Hume-Fogg School, of which McGaw was a graduate in 1931.

14. *WPA Guide to Tennessee*, compiled and written by the Federal Writers Project (1939;, reprint, New York: Viking, 1986), 122.

15. For a fuller account, see John Edwin Windrow, *John Berrien Lindsley: Educator, Physician, Social Philosopher* (Chapel Hill: University of North Carolina Press, 1938).

16. Margaret Lindsley Warden, "Louise Grundy Lindsley, 1858–1944," in *Seven Women of Nashville* (Nashville: Nashville Room, Public Library of Nashville & Davidson County, 1974), 75–86.

17. See Wooldridge, 399–405, and Alfred L. Crabb, *Nashville: Personality of a City* (New York: Bobbs-Merrill, 1960), 174.

18. Interview with Sister Benedict and Sister Rose Marie of St. Cecilia Academy, September 4, 1995. Wooldridge, 435, notes of the St. Cecilia curriculum in 1890: "The course of instruction embraces all the requisites of a thorough and accomplished education."

19. Wooldridge, 435.

20. Wooldridge, 438.

21. Herman Norton, *Religion in Tennessee 1777–1945* (Knoxville: University of Tennessee Press, 1981), 3–6.

22. Ernest Trice Thompson, *Presbyterians in the South,* vol. 1 *1607–1861* (Richmond: John Knox, 1963), 144.

23. Thompson, 145.

24. Ben Melton Barrus, A Study of the Factors Involved in the Origin of the Cumberland Presbyterian Church: 1800–1813, Ph.D. diss., Vanderbilt University, 1964, 157.

25. Barrus, 164.

26. Norton, 35–37.

27. Edward L. Wheeler, *Uplifting the Race: The Black Minister in the New South, 1865–1902* (Lanham, Md.: University Press of America, 1986), 111–112.

28. See Wheeler, 112.

29. Wheeler, 112.

30. Wheeler, 114.

31. Wheeler, 114.

32. *Fisk University Catalogue* (1906–1907), 14.

33. *Fisk University Catalogue* (1896–1897), 5.

34. See Joseph R. Berrigan, "Milton W. Humphreys: An Appalachian Odysseus," in *The Classical Tradition in the South*, ed. Susan Ford Wiltshire, *Southern Humanities Review* (special issue, 1977): 29–30.

35. Tate recalls affectionately Tolman's teaching of Pindar in "Several Thousand Books," *Sewanee Review* 75 (summer 1967): 380–381.

36. *Vanderbilt University Bulletin* (Nashville: Vanderbilt University Press, 1921), 47, 54, and 47.

37. Louise Cowan, *The Fugitive Group: A Literary History* (Baton Rouge: Louisiana State University, 1959), 33.

38. Paul K. Conkin, *The Southern Agrarians* (Knoxville: University of Tennessee Press, 1988), 4.

39. Don H. Doyle, *Nashville Since the 1920s* (Knoxville: University of Tennessee Press, 1985), 8. See also Doyle's discussion of the Fugitives generally, 4–10.

40. Reminiscence of Robert Penn Warren in John Egerton, *Nashville: The Faces of Two Centuries 1780–1980* (Nashville: PlusMedia, 1979), 206.

41. Donald Davidson, *Southern Writers in the Modern World* (Athens: University of Georgia Press, 1958), 8.

42. Cowan, xvi. "The Fugitives were a quite tangible body of sixteen poets who, having no particular program, met frequently from 1915 to 1928 for the purpose of reading and discussing their own work. The Agrarians were twelve scholars of various disciplines who, from about 1928 to 1935, were united by common principle rather than contiguity and whose intercommunications were conducted, for the most part, through letters and essays." The Agrarians Cowan lists are John Crowe Ransom, Donald Davidson, Allen Tate, Robert Penn Warren, Andrew Lytle, Stark Young, John Gould Fletcher, Frank Lawrence Owsley, Lyle Lanier, Henry Clarence Nixon, John Donald Wade, and Henry Blue Kline. The only overlapping members of the two groups were Davidson, Ransom, Tate, and Warren.

43. Allen Tate, "The Bi-Millennium of Vergil," *New Republic,* October 29, 1930, 298.

44. Radcliffe Squires, *Allen Tate, A Literary Biography* (New York: Pegasus, 1971), 118 and note 10. In a conversation with Susan Ford Wiltshire on April 14, 1978, Tate confirmed this sequences of events.

45. The line is from *Aeneid* 1.241. Vergil's text reads *laborum* for *dolorum*—labors instead of sufferings. When asked by Wiltshire during the April 14, 1978, interview about the variation, Tate said, "Oh, that was a typographical error."

46. Squires, 119.

47. Allen Tate, "Speculations," *Southern Review* 14 (1978): 227.

48. Arthur Mizener, in his introduction to Allen Tate, *The Fathers* (London: Eyre & Spottiswoode, 1960), xi.

49. Part of this discussion of *The Fathers* appears also in Susan Ford Wiltshire, "Vergil, Allen Tate, and the Analogy of Experience," *Classical and Modern Literature* 5, no.4 (winter 1985): 87–98.

50. Allen Tate in a letter to Donald Davidson, dated 20 February 1927, in *The Literary Correspondence of Donald Davidson and Allen Tate*, ed. John

Tyree Fain and Thomas Daniel Young (Athens: University of Georgia Press, 1974), 189.

51. Allen Tate to Donald Davidson, *The Literary Correspondence of Allen Tate and Donald Davidson*, 184.

52. Quoted by William Bedford Clark, *The American Vision of Robert Penn Warren*, (Lexington: University Press of Kentucky, 1991), 14.

53. Hugh Moore Jr., *Robert Penn Warren and History: The Big Myth We Live* (The Hague: Mouton, 1970), 150.

54. Robert Penn Warren, *Wilderness: A Tale of the Civil War* (New York: Random House, 1961), 96.

55. Moore, 151.

56. Moore, 21–22 and 182.

57. Robert Penn Warren, *A Place to Come To* (New York: Random House, 1977), 31.

58. Warren, *A Place to Come To*, 62.

59. Warren, *A Place to Come To*, 125.

CHAPTER II

1. Berman, Eleanor Davidson, *Thomas Jefferson Among the Arts: An Essay in Early American Esthetics* (New York: Philosophical Society, 1947), 114–115.

2. Lois A. Craig, *The Federal Presence: Architecture, Politics, and Symbols* (Cambridge: Massachusetts Institute of Technology Press, 1978), 23.

3. Bates Lowrey, *Building a National Image: Drawings for the American Democracy, 1789–1912* (Washington, D.C.: National Building Museum, 1985), 10–16.

4. Craig, Introduction, 23.

5. Lowrey, 10–26.

6. Craig, 52–55.

7. James Patrick, *Architecture in Tennessee, 1768–1897* (Knoxville: University of Tennessee Press, 1981), 101–102.

8. Patrick, 102. Patrick's fig. 113 illustrates this bank, which was probably the earliest temple-form building in Nashville.

9. Patrick, 31–32.

10. Patrick, 85–96, figs. 80, 81, 82.

11. An architectural form resembling the design of a Roman circular temple. Bramante's famous high Renaissance tempietto in the cloister of San Pietro Montorio in Rome is an example.

12. A full discussion of the significance of this commission is found in Nell Savage Mahoney, "William Strickland and the Building of Tennessee's Capitol, 1845–1854," *Tennessee Historical Quarterly* 4 (June 1945): 99–153.

13. William Strickland's letter of May 20, 1845, to the Commissioners for the Building of the State Capitol submitting his design proposal contains two references to the "cupola" and "Corinthian Tower," clearly contradicting persistent legend that it was a later addition. (*Senate Journal*, 1845–1846).

14. Clayton B. Dekle, "The Tennessee State Capitol," *Tennessee Historical Quarterly* 25, no. 3 (fall 1966): 3.

15. Stylistic similarity of the church's Ionic portico (see Patrick, 134, fig. 150), to those of the State Capitol suggests Strickland's influence.

16. Patrick, 140, quotes George Tucker, *Essays on Various Subjects of Taste, Morals and National Policy* (Georgetown, D.C.: the author, 1822): "Whether

the rules of art must ever remain stationary, or whether an uncontrollable thirst for novelty, may not hereafter embody some of the infinite diversity of untried forms; and having overleaped the bounds which have hitherto checked the luxuriant wanderings of taste, at length incessantly effect capricious novelties, it is for time only to show."

17. *Art Work of Nashville 1894–1901* (1894; reprint, Nashville: Tennessee Historical Society, 1981 contains numerous photographs and histories of late nineteenth-century buildings, most of which are in the various recognized architectural styles, but some of whose stylistic origins can only be guessed at.

18. Lowrey, 72–75.

19. See Lowrey's general discussion, 52–71.

20. Nelson Bryan, "The Distinguished Ancestry of the Social Religious Building," *Peabody Reflector* 64, no. 1 (summer 1993), 8–9.

21. Henry-Russell Hitchcock and Philip Johnson, *The International Style* (1932; reprint, New York: Norton, 1966), 13–14.

22. Craig, 282, 294.

CHAPTER III

1. Ridley Wills II, *The History of Belle Meade: Mansion, Plantation, and Stud* (Nashville: Vanderbilt University Press, 1991), 5.

2. Carol Rifkind, *A Field Guide to American Architecture* (New York: New American Library, 1980), 39.

3. Michael Greenhalgh, *What Is Classicism?* (New York: St. Martin's, 1990), 11.

4. Greenhalgh, 10.

5. Greenhalgh, 8.

6. Greenhalgh, 10.

7. James Patrick, *Architecture in Tennessee: 1768–1897* (1981; reprint, Knoxville: University of Tennessee Press, 1990), 121. The date of the additions is given as the 1840s in Paul Clements, *A Past Remembered: a Collection of Antebellum Houses in Davidson County* (Nashville: Clearview, 1987), 178.

8. Interview with Barbara Tsakirgis, by Christine Kreyling, February 10, 1995.

9. Michelangelo Muraro, *Venetian Villas: The History and Culture* (New York: Rizzoli, 1986), 61.

10. Greenhalgh, 19.

11. This summary of the path of classicism is from Greenhalgh, 21.

12. Don Creighton Gifford, "The Confluence of Ideas," *The Literature of Architecture* (New York: E. P. Dutton, 1966), 64.

13. Mills Lane, *Architecture of the Old South* (New York: Abbeville, 1993), 66.

14. Kenneth Severens, *Southern Architecture: 350 Years of Distinctive American Buildings* (New York: E. P. Dutton, 1981), 82.

15. Severens, 82.

16. Thomas Jefferson, letter to James Madison, September 20, 1785; quoted in Severens, 84.

17. Severens, 85, 89.

18. No trained architect has ever been linked to Mount Vernon; Washington's own training as a surveyor enabled him to make measured

drawings.

19. Roger G. Kennedy, *Greek Revival America* (New York: Stewart, Tabori & Chang, 1989), 64.

20. Quoted in Severens, 80.

21. Stanley Horn, *The Hermitage: Home of Old Hickory* (New York: Greenberg, 1950), 22.

22. Patrick, 121.

23. Patrick, 123.

24. Patrick, 173.

25. Patrick, 170.

26. Severens, 118.

27. Quoted in Albert W. Wardin Jr., *Belmont Mansion: the Home of Joseph and Adelicia Acklen* (Nashville: Historic Belmont Association, 1981), 27.

28. For definition and application of the "picuresque" in settings like Belmont, see Sue Rainey, *Creating Picturesque America: Monument of the Natural and Cultural Landscape* (Nashville: Vanderbilt University Press, 1994), especially chapters 2 and 6.

29. Quoted in Severens, 117.

30. Quoted in Wardin, 16.

31. Gifford, "Reaction in America," in *The Literature of Architecture*, 550–551

32. Quoted in Wardin, 20.

33. Interview with Ann Reynolds, by Christine Kreyling, November 12, 1995.

CHAPTER IV

1. Herman Justi, ed., *The Official History of the Tennessee Centennial Exposition* (Nashville: Brandon Printing, 1898), 14.

2. Justi, p. 32.

3. Wilbur F. Creighton Jr., and Leland R. Johnson, *The Parthenon in Nashville: Athens of the South,* revised edition (Nashville: JM Productions, 1989), 15.

4. Justi, 112.

5. Creighton, 16–17.

6. Creighton, 24.

7. Justi, 22.

8. Justi, 120.

9. William Bell Dinsmoor, *The Architecture of Ancient Greece,* 3d. edition, revised (1950; reprint, New York: Norton, 1975), 164.

10. Susan Woodford, *The Parthenon* (Cambridge: Cambridge University Press, 1981), 27. For a detailed discussion of the unique nature and quality of the architectural refinements of the Parthenon, see Manolis Korres, "The Architecture of the Parthenon," in *The Parthenon and Its Impact in Modern Times,* ed. Panayotis Tournikiotes (Athens: Melissa, 1994).

11. Creighton, 28.

12. Ann Reynolds, "Nashville's Parthenon as Symbol," (unpublished, 1993), 13.

13. Justi, 474.

14. Charles B. Castner, "Tennessee's Biggest Birthday Party," typescript for *L & N Magazine* (April 1967), pages not numbered.

15. James Patrick, *Architecture in Tennessee* (Knoxville: University of

Tennessee Press, 1981), 118.

16. Justi, 112–113.

17. Justi, 1.

18. Justi, 14.

19. Justi, 14.

20. Jeffrey M. Hurwit, "Beautiful Evil: Pandora and the Athena Parthenos," *American Journal of Archaeology* 90 (April 1995): 182.

21. Paul Goldberger, "Grand Old Athens in the Land of Grand Old Opry," *New York Times,* March 5, 1989, H 35.

CONCLUSION

1. William Doreski, *The Years of Our Friendship: Robert Lowell and Allen Tate* (Jackson: University Press of Mississippi, 1990), 139.

2. Interviewed by Angela Wibking in *Nashville Business Journal,* July 24–28, 1995, 15.

3. See Paul K. Conkin, *Gone with the Ivy: A Biography of Vanderbilt University* (Knoxville: University of Tennessee Press, 1985), 314 and 486 for discussions of the study of classics at Vanderbilt. In the 1920s, Vanderbilt students completed over half of their required courses in the study of Latin, Greek, and English.

4. Interview with John Hope Franklin by Susan Ford Wiltshire, November 17, 1995.

5. John Hope Franklin, "An Educational Awakening," in John Egerton, *Nashville: The Faces of Two Centuries* (Nashville: PlusMedia Incorporated, 1979), 111.

6. Donald Davidson, *Poems 1922–1961* (Minneapolis: University of Minnesota Press, 1966), 64.

7. Thomas Daniel Young and M. Thomas Inge, *Donald Davidson* (New York: Twayne, 1971), 96–97.

8. Richard A. Peterson, "Getting Beyond the 'Athens Idea,'" in *Nashville: Its Character in a Changing America,* ed. Robert L. Mode (Nashville: Vanderbilt University Office of University Publications, 1981), 77–84, especially 81–82.

9. Allen Tate, "Remarks on Southern Religion," in *I'll Take My Stand: The South an d the Agrarian Tradition*, by Twelve Southerners (New York: Harper & Brothers, 1930), 156.

10. Barbara Mann, "Local Education and the Challenge of Diversity," in *Nashville: Its Character in a Changing America,* 71.

11. Nikos Kazantzakis, *The Odyssey: A Modern Sequel*, trans. and ed. Kimon Friar (New York: Simon and Schuster, 1958), xxvi.

Bibliography

Adams, George Rollie and Ralph Jerry Christian. *Nashville, A Pictorial History*. Virginia Beach: Downing, n.d.

Art Work of Nashville 1894–1901. 1894. Reprint, Tennessee Historical Society, 1981.

Barrus, Ben Melton. *A Study of the Factors Involved in the Origin of the Cumberland Presbyterian Church: 1800–1813*. Ph.D. diss., Vanderbilt University, 1964.

Beard, William E. *First Presbyterian Church of Nashville: 100 Years of Service*. Nashville: Foster & Parkes Company, 1915.

Benedict, Burton. *The Anthropology of World's Fairs: San Francisco's Panama Pacific International Exposition of 1915*. Berkeley, Calif.: Scolar, 1983.

Berman, Eleanor Davidson. *Thomas Jefferson among the Arts: An Essay in Early American Esthetics*. New York: Philosophical Library, 1947.

Berrigan, Joseph R. "Milton W. Humphreys: An Appalachian Odysseus." In *The Classical Tradition in the South*. Edited by Susan Ford Wiltshire. *Southern Humanities Review* (special issue, 1977).

Brumbaugh, Thomas B. *Architecture of Middle Tennessee*. Nashville: Vanderbilt University Press, 1974.

Bryan, Nelson. "The Distinguished Ancestry of the Social Religious Building." *Peabody Reflector* 64, no. 1 (summer 1993): 8–9.

Castner, Charles B. "Tennessee's Biggest Birthday Party," typescript for *L & N Magazine*. (April, 1967).

Cigliano, Jan and Sarah Bedford Landau, eds. *The Grand American Avenue: 1850–1920*. San Francisco: Pomegranate Artbooks, in association with the Octagon, the Museum of the American Architectural Foundation, 1994.

Clark, T. J. *The Painting of Modern Life*. Princeton, N.J.: Princeton University Press, 1984.

Clark, William Bedford. *The American Vision of Robert Penn Warren*. Lexington: University Press of Kentucky, 1991.

Clayton, W. W. *History of Davidson County, Tennessee*. Philadelphia: J. W. Lewis, 1880.

Clements, Paul. *A Past Remembered: a Collection of Antebellum Houses in Davidson County*. Nashville: Clearview, 1987.

Cochran, Gifford A. *Grandeur in Tennessee*. New York: J. J. Augustin, 1946.

Conkin, Paul K. *Gone with the Ivy: A Biography of Vanderbilt University*. Knoxville: University of Tennessee Press, 1985.

———. *The Southern Agrarians*. Knoxville: University of Tennessee Press, 1988.

Constitution of the State of Tennessee. Nashville: Division of Publications, Department of State, 1982.

Cowan, Louise. *The Fugitive Group: A Literary History*. Baton Rouge: Louisiana State University, 1959.

Crabb, Alfred L. *Nashville: Personality of a City*. New York: Bobbs-Merrill, 1960.

Craig, Lois A. *The Federal Presence: Architecture, Politics, and Symbols*. Cambridge: Massachusetts Institutes of Technology Press, 1978.

Crane, William Carey. *Life and Select Literary Remains of Sam Houston of Texas*. Philadelphia: J. B. Lippincott, 1884.

Creighton, Wilbur F. Jr., and Leland R. Johnson. *The Parthenon in Nashville: Athens of the South*. Revised edition. Nashville: JM Productions, 1989.

Davidson, Donald. *Poems 1922–1961*. Minneapolis: University of Minnesota Press, 1966.

———. *Southern Writers in the Modern World*. Athens: University of Georgia Press, 1958.

Davidson, Donald, and Allen Tate. *The Literary Correspondence of Donald Davidson and Allen Tate*. Edited by John Tyree Fain and Thomas Daniel Young. Athens: University of Georgia Press, 1974.

Dekle, Clayton B. Dekle. "The Tennessee State Capitol." *Tennessee Historical Quarterly* 25 no. 3 (fall, 1966): 213–238.

Dinsmoor, William Bell. *The Architecture of Ancient Greece*. 3d. edition, revised. 1950. Reprint, New York: Norton, 1975.

Doreski, William. *The Years of Our Friendship: Robert Lowell and Allen Tate*. Jackson: University Press of Mississippi, 1990.

Doyle, Don H. *Nashville in the New South: 1880–1930*. Knoxville: University of Tennessee Press, 1985.

———. *Nashville Since the 1920s*. Knoxville: University of Tennessee Press, 1985.

Egerton, John. "Athens of the West? A little culture went a long way in creating image." *Society of Professional Journalists.* 1994 Convention.

———. *Nashville, The Faces of Two Centuries 1780–1980.* Nashville: PlusMedia Incorporated, 1979.

Fisk University Catalogue. Nashville: Fisk University, 1896–1897; 1906–1907.

Fletcher, Banister. *A History of Architecture.* New York: Charles Scribner's Sons, 1975.

Friend, Llerena. "Sam Houston—Bio-bibliographical." *Texas Grand Lodge Magazine* (March 1957): 113–118.

Gifford, Don Creighton, ed. *The Literature of Architecture.* New York: E. P. Dutton, 1966.

Gilchrist, Agnes Addison. *William Strickland, Architect and Engineer.* Philadelphia: University of Pennsylvania Press, 1950.

Goldberger, Paul. "Grand Old Athens in the Land of Grand Old Opry." *New York Times*, March 5, 1989.

Goodstein, Anita Shafer. *Nashville, 1780–1860: From Frontier to City.* Gainesville: University Press of Florida, 1989.

Graham, Eleanor, ed. *Nashville: A Short History and Selected Buildings.* Nashville: Historical Commission of Metropolitan Nashville-Davidson County, 1974.

Greenhalgh, Michael. *What Is Classicism?* New York: St. Martin's, 1990.

Halsey, Leroy J. *A Sketch of the Life and Educational Labors of Philip Lindsley, D.D.* Hartford: Williams, Wiley & Turner, 1859. Reprinted from *Barnard's American Journal of Education* (September, 1859).

———, ed. *The Works of Philip Lindsley.* Philadelphia: J. B. Lippincott, 1866.

Hitchcock, Henry-Russell, and Philip Johnson. *The International Style.* 1932. Reprint, New York: Norton, 1966.

Horn, Stanley. *The Hermitage, Home of Old Hickory.* New York: Greenberg, 1950.

Hurwit, Jeffrey M. "Beautiful Evil: Pandora and the Athena Parthenos," *American Journal of Archaeology* 90 (April 1995): 171–186.

I'll Take my Stand: The South and the Agrarian Tradition, by Twelve Southerners. New York: Harper & Brothers, 1930.

Justi, Herman, ed.. *The Official History of the Tennessee Centennial Exposition.* Nashville: Brandon, 1898.

Kazantzakis, Nikos. *The Odyssey: A Modern Sequel.* Translated and edited by Kimon Friar. New York: Simon & Schuster, 1958.

Kennedy, Roger G. *Architecture, Men, Women and Money in America:*

1600–1860. New York: Random House, 1985.

———. *Greek Revival America*. New York: Stewart, Tabori & Chang; dist. Workman, 1989.

Korres, Manolis. "The Architecture of the Parthenon," *The Parthenon and Its Impact in Modern Times*. Athens: Melissa, 1994.

Lafever, Minard. *The Modern Builder's Guide*. 1833. Reprint, New York: Dover, 1969.

Lane, Mills. *Architecture of the Old South*. New York: Abbeville, 1993.

Lester, Charles. *Life and Achievements of Sam Houston, Hero and Statesman*. New York: J. B. Alden, 1883.

Lowrey, Bates. *Building a National Image: Architectural Drawings for the American Democracy, 1789–1912*. Washington: National Building Museum, 1985.

Mahoney, Nell Savage. "William Strickland and the Building of Tennessee's Capitol, 1845–1854." *Tennessee Historical Quarterly* 4 (June 1945): 99–153.

McGaw, Robert A. "Hume-Fogg Remembered." Paper presented to the Old Oak Club, Nashville, Tennessee, December 2, 1992.

McRaven, Henry. *Nashville: Athens of the South*. Chapel Hill: Scheer & Jervis, 1949.

Mode, Robert L., ed. *Nashville: Its Character in a Changing America*. Nashville: Vanderbilt University Office of University Publications, 1981.

Moore, L. Hugh, Jr. *Robert Penn Warren and History: The Big Myth We Live*. The Hague: Mouton, 1970.

Muraro, Michelangelo. *Venetian Villas: The History and Culture*. New York: Rizzoli, 1986.

Norton, Herman. *Religion in Tennessee 1777–1945*. Knoxville: University of Tennessee Press, 1981.

Patrick, James. *Architecture in Tennessee*. Knoxville, University of Tennessee Press, 1981.

Rainey, Sue. *Creating* Picturesque America: *Monument to the Natural and Cultural Landscape*. Nashville: Vanderbilt University Press, 1994.

Ramsey, J. G. M. *The Annals of Tennessee to the End of the Eighteenth Century*. 1853. Reprint, Kingsport, Tenn.: Kingsport, 1926.

Reynolds, Ann. "Nashville's Parthenon As Symbol." unpublished, 1993.

Rifkind, Carol. *A Field Guide to American Architecture*. New York: New American Library, 1980.

Roth, Leland M. *A Concise History of American Architecture*. New York: Harper & Row, 1979.

Scully, Vincent. *Architecture: The Natural and the Manmade*. New York: St. Martin's, 1991.

Scully, Vincent and Philip Trager. *The Villas of Palladio*. 1986. Reprint, Boston: Little, Brown, 1992.

Severens, Kenneth. *Southern Architecture: 350 Years of Distinctive American Buildings*. New York: E. P. Dutton, 1981.

Sloane, David Charles. *The Last Great Necessity : Cemeteries in American History*. Baltimore: Johns Hopkins University Press, 1991.

Squires, Radcliffe. *Allen Tate: A Literary Biography*. New York: Pegasus, 1971.

Stilgoe, John. *Borderland: Origins of the American Suburb, 1820–1939*. New Haven, Conn.: Yale University Press, 1988.

Stuart, James and Nicholas Revett. *The Antiquities of Athens, Measured and Delineated*. Facsimile of the original edition of 1762–94. New York: Benjamin Blom, 1968.

Tate, Allen. "The Bi-Millenium of Vergil." *New Republic,* October 29, 1930.

———. *The Fathers*. Edited by Arthur Mizener. London: Eyre & Spottiswood, 1960.

———. "Several Thousand Books." *Sewanee Review* 75 (Summer 1967): 377–384.

———. "Speculations." *Southern Review* 14 (spring 1978): 226–232.

Thompson, Ernest Trice. *Presbyterians in the South,* vol. 1, *1607–1861*. Richmond: John Knox, 1963.

Three Pioneer Tennessee Documents. Nashville: The Tennessee Historical Commission, 1964.

Vanderbilt University Bulletin. Nashville: Vanderbilt University Press, 1921.

Warden, Margaret Lindsley. "Louise Grundy Lindsley, 1858–1944." *Seven Women of Nashville*. Nashville: Nashville Room, Public Library of Nashville & Davidson County, 1974.

Wardin, Albert W., Jr. *Belmont Mansion: The Home of Joseph and Adelicia Acklen*. Nashville: Historic Belmont Association, 1981.

Warren, Robert Penn. *How Texas Won Her Freedom: The Story of Sam Houston and the Battle of San Jacinto*. San Jacinto Monument, Tex.: 1958.

———. *A Place to Come to*. New York: Random House, 1977.

———. *Wilderness: A Tale of the Civil War*. New York: Random House, 1961.

Wheeler, Edward L. *Uplifting the Race: The Black Minister in the New South, 1865–1902*. Lanham, Md.: University Press of America, 1986.

Wills, Jesse. *Nashville and Other Poems*. Nashville: Fantasie, 1973.

Wills, Ridley, II. *The History of Belle Meade: Mansion, Plantation, and Stud*. Nashville: Vanderbilt University Press, 1991.

Wiltshire, Susan Ford. "Vergil, Allen Tate, and the Analogy of Experience." *Classical and Modern Literature* 5, no.4 (winter 1985).

———. "Sam Houston and the *Iliad*." *Tennessee Historical Quarterly* 32 (fall 1979).

Windrow, John Edwin. *John Berrien Lindsley: Educator, Physician, Social Philosopher*. Chapel Hill: University of North Carolina Press, 1938.

Woodford, Susan. *The Parthenon*. Cambridge: Cambridge University Press, 1981.

Wooldridge, John, ed. *History of Nashville, Tenn.* Nashville: Publishing House of the Methodist Episcopal Church, South, 1890.

WPA Guide to Tennessee. Compiled and written by the Federal Writers Project. 1939. Reprint, New York: Viking, 1986.

Young, Thomas Daniel and M. Thomas Inge. *Donald Davidson*. New York: Twayne, 1971.

About the Authors

Christine Kreyling is an architecture and urban planning critic. A series of her articles for the *Nashville Scene* received a journalism award from the American Planning Association for Best Writing in the Country for a mid-sized newspaper. Kreyling contributes articles on art and architecture to *Boulevard* magazine, *Nashville Life*, and *Architecture* magazine. Currently she is preparing a catalog for an exhibition on the sculpture of Nashville native William Edmondson and is pursuing graduate study in the history of art and architecture at Vanderbilt University.

Wesley Paine has been director of the Nashville Parthenon since 1979. Earlier she was director for five years of Fort Nashborough. Paine studied Museum Administration at the University of Oklahoma. She has provided a regular art commentary for the Channel 5 program "Talk of the Town." Paine is also a founding board member of Theatre Parthenos, in one of whose productions she appeared as Athena.

Charles W. Warterfield, Jr., FAIA, has been in the private practice of architecture in Nashville since 1960. A graduate of Vanderbilt University and the Yale School of Architecture, he served his apprenticeship as chief draftsman for the restoration of the Tennessee State Capitol in 1955–1957. In 1987–1988 Warterfield was in charge of the interior restoration of the Capitol. Having served as a member of the Master Planning Team for the design of the Bicentennial Mall, he is now principal-in-charge of the restoration of the grounds and historic features of the State Capitol.

Susan Ford Wiltshire is professor of Classics at Vanderbilt University. She is the author of *Public and Private in Vergil's Aeneid* (University of Massachusetts Press, 1989) and *Greece, Rome, and the Bill of Rights* (University of Oklahoma Press, 1992), which received the Alex Haley Memorial Award for Literary Distinction in 1993. She edited *The Usefulness of Classical Learning in the Eighteenth Century* (American Philological Association, 1977) and "The Classical Tradition in the South," *Southern Humanities Review* (1977).

■

Nashville sculptor *Alan LeQuire,* after his graduation from Vanderbilt in 1978, became an apprentice to Milton Hebald, an American sculptor living in Italy. Upon his return to the United States in 1980, he completed the Master of Fine Arts degree at the University of North Carolina-Greensboro. In 1981 he competed for and won the commission to re-create the lost *Athena Parthenos* by Pheidias for the Parthenon in Nashville. Since 1980 his commissioned works have included *David* for the Blair School of Music, a three-figure monumental bronze Viet Nam Memorial, and many portraits in bronze and other media.

An award-winning book designer, *Gary Gore* is the director of the Department of Publications and Design at Vanderbilt University. Among his recognitions for outstanding book-design work are four *50 Books of the Year* awards, including one for *The Architecture of Middle Tennessee* (Vanderbilt University Press, 1971). In addition, a one-man show of his book jackets was displayed by the American Institute of Graphic Arts in its New York gallery. Gore has written a number of articles on book design for such journals as *The Inland Printer, Publishers Weekly,* and *Scholarly Publishing.*

Index

(Bold-face numbers indicate illustrations)

Ward-Belmont, 12
Warden, Margaret Lindsley, 156
Warfield & Keeble
    (architectural firm), 69–70
Warfield, Francis B., 70
Warren, Robert Penn, xiii, xvi,
    4, 22; *Wilderness*, 27–29; *A
    Place to Come To*, 27, 29–31
Warterfield, Charles W., Jr., 10
Washington College (now
    Washington and Lee
    University), 19
Washington, Booker T., 16
Washington, George, 34, 103;
    and architecture of Mount
    Vernon, 92–95, 96, 100, 167
    n. 18; and plan of District of
    Columbia, 35
West End Avenue, 112–13, 114;
    residences, **112**, **113**
Western Military Institute, 9
Westminster Presbyterian

Church, 69–70, **73**
Whalen, James, 11
Wheeler, Edward, 15, 16
Whitehead, Alfred North, 145
Williams, Roger, 17
Williamsburg, Virginia, 33
Wills, Jesse, 1, 10, 22
Wills, Ridley, 22
Wilson & Odom (architectural
    firm), 74
Woodford, Susan, 129–30
Woodland Presbyterian
    Church, 58, **59**
Woolwine, Emmons, 67
World War I, 20, 21, 22, 62–63
World War II, 68–69, 152
Wright, Frank Lloyd, 56

Xenophon, 20

Young, T. Daniel, 157